100
Ways to
Publish and
Sell Your Own
E-Book
– and make it a bestseller

Other related titles from How To Books

LIKELY STORIES
Fabulous, inspirational, chuckleworthy and deeeply instructive tales about creative writing as told to the author by his ubiquitous Guru
Hugh Scott
Whitbread winning author

365 WAYS TO GET YOU WRITING
Daily inspiration and advice for creative writers
Jane Cooper

CHOOSE THE RIGHT WORD
An entertaining and easy-to-use guide to better English – with 70 test yourself quizzes
Robin Hosie & Vic Mayhew

THE JOY OF ENGLISH
100 illuminating conversations about the English language
Jesse Karjalainen

HOW TO WRITE YOUR FIRST NOVEL
Sophie King

THE FIVE-MINUTE WRITER
Exercise and inspiration in creative writing in five minutes a day
Margret Geraghty

100 Ways to Publish and Sell Your Own E-Book

– and make it a bestseller

Conrad Jones and Darin Jewell

howtobooks

Constable & Robinson Ltd
55–56 Russell Square
London WC1B 4HP
www.constablerobinson.com

First published in the UK by How To Books,
an imprint of Constable & Robinson Ltd, 2013

A copy of the British Library Cataloguing in
Publication Data is available from the British Library

ISBN 978-1-84528-507-4

Printed and bound in the UK

1 3 5 7 9 10 8 6 4 2

This book is dedicated to Aidan Jewell and Aimee Jewell

Contents

About the Authors

CONRAD JONES

Conrad started writing as a business venture. It was a change of career, not an artistic project. Although he eventually achieved a respectable income from his books, things were not simple in the beginning and he learned some harsh lessons along the way. Based on his varied experiences in selling and promoting his own e-books, Conrad explains to authors the things that worked and the things that didn't. He had no agent to start with and no publisher to guide and support his efforts. Rather, he learned the hard way, through trial and error.

It was a back-to-front journey but the success of his e-book sales earned him the interest of a good agent and a publishing deal. If you can follow the simple guidelines and tips set out in this book then you can build sales and prove to the traditional industry that you are a saleable asset in the literary world. Or, if you prefer, you can choose to go it alone and still make a decent residual monthly income.

When Conrad turned his paperbacks into e-books, his thriller series stormed the Kindle charts. Within three weeks of launching them, he had two titles (*The Child Taker* and *Slow Burn*) in the top ten Kindle lists. Not genre lists, the overall sales chart. All seven of his thrillers were in the top forty for nearly twelve months. On the release of his eighth book (*Nine Angels*), it flew to number three in the horror charts overnight. *The Child Taker* was number one in thriller law books and *Tank* was number one in thriller war books. He achieved over 120,000 digital downloads in the first year. It wasn't just luck. Rather, it was the success of building a marketing base over a period of years and then applying everything that he had learned to the launch of his e-books. His credentials are actual book sales, a growing fan base and over 250 five-star reviews across the *Soft Target* series.

DARIN JEWELL

Darin Jewell is Director of The Inspira Group Literary Agency in London. Born in the USA, Darin settled in the UK in the early 1990s. He published *How to Sell & Market Your Book* in 2010 which tells authors how to raise their literary profile and promote their books in easy and effective ways. It sets out the resources available and outlines which paths are likely to sell the most number of copies and which will establish the writer as a published author, and as a marketable and commercial brand name.

As director of a professional UK literary agency, he receives hundreds of requests for representation from authors each month and regularly participates as a panellist in writing seminars and speaks to various writing groups each year. He advises authors on how they can drive and manage each stage of the publishing process for their books from production to pricing right through to promotion.

Darin has placed over a hundred books in the last decade with traditional publishers and represents Michael G. R. Tolkien, Kevin Joslin, David Barry, best-selling business book author Fergus O'Connell, best-selling humour writer Mark Leigh, best-selling e-book author Conrad Jones and Mind, Body, Spirit (MBS) author Simon Brown whose *Feng Shui* book has sold over a million copies to date.

Introduction

SETTING REALISTIC SALES TARGETS

Most of the tips and processes in this guide are used on a daily basis by successful authors and publishers. Because of the internet, we are in a position to reach and touch millions of readers across the globe and if you can grasp the basics and use them regularly then you will sell your books. Marketing is a relentless but essential part of publishing. To be successful, you need to set aside time every working day to update your profile, assess reviews, social network and monitor sales and promotions.

To set sales targets and plan a marketing strategy it is useful to know how established brands achieve this. In my previous career, I was area manager for McDonald's Restaurants. I worked for twelve years progressing from trainee manager to senior management. You may not be aware that each individual restaurant is held accountable for its sales increases or decreases on a daily, weekly, monthly and yearly basis.

This constant monitoring of each individual restaurant's growth and profitability was integral to their success. As a store manager, you are encouraged to market your restaurant locally and believe me I've seen some amazingly simple ideas turn declining restaurants into goldmines. That is where I learned about marketing on a local, regional and global scale. McDonald's is one of the most successful and recognisable brands on the planet and you can emulate them by working on a daily basis to raise your literary profile and build up your author name as a recognised brand. It's as easy as PIE: **P**lan, **I**mplement and **E**valuate.

As an author without the backing of a big publisher, book marketing is your number one priority but many authors find that sitting down and planning a marketing campaign is alien to them. I am not going to tell you that it is easy because it isn't but if you follow the core basics, you will develop your marketing skills alongside your writing.

You have to dedicate as much time and effort to selling your book as you did in writing it. To make it more approachable, let's break it down into areas we can look at individually. You have to separate them to plan them effectively. Once we have looked at the basics of marketing, you should have a complete overview of what's involved in successfully marketing your book and allowing it to reach its full potential, without breaking the bank. Some of the e-book marketing tips in this book are case specific but they may provoke ideas which you can adapt to your circumstances.

It's important that we're realistic about potential sales that can be reasonably achieved and that we set challenging but achievable targets. Every reader has their favourite authors and genres. Few James Herbert fans will have rushed out to buy *Fifty Shades of Grey*. If your book has a potential readership then finding them and letting them know that your book is available is the key to selling it. Once it is selling, your readers will soon let you know if it is any good or not!

The most important element in book marketing is not how much money you have to throw at a promotional campaign; it is the drive and commitment of the individual author and the commercial potential of the book itself. If your book is full of dross, then it simply won't sell. If it's about thermonuclear-physics in the bathroom or it is a collection of poems that have special meaning to you, then your market is limited. That doesn't mean no one will buy it, but you need to be realistic about sales projections.

The majority of self-published print-on-demand novels sell less than 200 copies. Of course, there have been exceptions but that is your first goal. Beat the average and you have succeeded. If your book is good, then you will beat that sales figure in your first campaign. There are several different measures of what constitutes a bestseller. In the main, 10,000 copies in the first twelve months or 15,000 in total can be classed as bestsellers while other gurus have moved the yard-stick to 35,000 copies. The point that I want to make is that these are largely variable figures and success is relative to the format, pricing and promotional support.

WRITING A BEST-SELLING BOOK

Why do some books fly off the shelves while others flounder? Sometimes it is simply timing but mostly it is the quality of the product which drives sales through word of mouth or 'viral' marketing. There are thousands of great storylines and plots that have floundered because the editing and proof reading isn't up to scratch. You should do all that you can to avoid writing defects in your book, because a book that is poorly edited, hard to read or difficult to position within the market is going to meet significant obstacles finding a wide readership.

Make sure your book conforms to generally-accepted editing and design standards so you don't cripple your own marketing efforts. Do not rely on one set of eyes to proof read your novel, especially your own. You will only read what you think you have written. You will find a UK Grammatical Guide in Appendix 2 of this book.

Quality books will give you a return on your marketing investment because once other people learn about the product, they are much more likely to buy it and recommend it to others. Endorsements and positive reviews from your readers is the biggest seller of books. Look at *Neuromancer* by William Gibson which came from a little-known author as his debut book to sell millions of copies and win the science-fiction 'triple crown' – the Nebula Award, the Philip K. Dick Award, and the Hugo Award.

How many times did avid sci-fi readers recommend this book on specialist fantasy and sci-fi discussion boards, in sci-fi e-zines and on Goodreads and Lovereading websites, and why did their reviews make such an impact in the book charts?

Similarly, why has *The Da Vinci Code* sold in excess of eighty million copies worldwide? The reason is clear. Dan Brown insinuated that Jesus had a living bloodline and that the Virgin was buried beneath the inverted pyramid at the Louvre. That got tongues wagging! The fiction was so cleverly entwined in the facts that many people believed the hype and had to read it for themselves.

Fifty Shades of Grey is hot and steamy and it had women intrigued as to how pornographic it really was, but the key to all three of these books in different genres is that people raved about them to other people. There's nothing like a good recommendation to help sell your book, and good recommendations come from well-written and professionally edited books.

Why mention these books in particular? Because all three of these books were in print and available for a while before they took off. Word of mouth or 'viral marketing' as it is commonly referred to within literary circles, and word of mouse or 'social networking' as it is commonly known, launched these novels because they were appealing and once people started talking about them online and offline, they sold millions.

There are many reasons why different kinds of books sell, and we can identify a few clear reasons why some sell better than others as follows.

+ It is unique and has current information that's in demand, but that cannot be found anywhere else.

+ It has a story which is compelling and entertaining.

+ The author is a well-known celebrity or a well-established author with a large following.

+ The book sells well and as sales grow, people start talking about it and telling others about the book.

I am guessing that not many celebrities or their ghostwriters are going to buy this book so I'll rule that one out for now. Only you and the readers can decide if your story is compelling and entertaining, so your goal is get people talking about you and your book.

This last point is the ultimate goal of our marketing efforts. No one will raise a huge flag and launch fireworks for you when you upload your book and you cannot force people to buy it, no matter how much money you spend on advertising or how many times you appear in the newspapers or on radio shows. They have no longevity. Influencing people in an endearing manner is the key to gaining interest over a prolonged period. A friend or colleague at work who tells you that you 'have to read this book' is a far more powerful marketing tool than any other.

You have to begin building a brand from day one and this book explains how to make people remember you as well as your books. You want every reader you meet to hear about your book and to tell their friends about your story as well as the titles of your other books.

HOW TO BUILD A BRAND NAME

You need to market yourself as well as your book, which means communicating the message that you want others to hear about your books to a plethora of audiences over a sustained period of time. You have dedicated time and effort into spreading the word, growing your brand and converting readers into fans who will tell their friends and buy your next book.

Branding is something people hear a lot about but don't fully understand how complex it can be. Examples of good branding are BMW, Microsoft and Virgin. If you buy a product with its brand name on it, you are expecting it to be reliable and great quality. If you shop for beans at Aldi or Lidl, you know the products will be good but perhaps not the same quality as beans from Sainsbury's.

A well-known example of poor branding is when Gerald Ratner, the Chief Executive of the once profitable Ratners Group of jewellers made a speech at the Institute of Directors in London in April 1991, and commented:

> We do cut-glass sherry decanters complete with six glasses on a silver-plated tray that your butler can serve you drinks on, all for £4.95.

People say, 'How can you sell this for such a low price?' I say, 'Because it's total crap.'

He compounded this by going on to remark that some of the earrings were 'Cheaper than an M&S prawn sandwich but probably wouldn't last as long.'

Ratner's comments are textbook examples of how you can alienate your target market with substandard quality and off-the-cuff remarks. Consumers exacted their revenge by staying away from Ratner shops. The value of Ratners Group plummeted by £500 million, which nearly lead to the company's collapse. Ratner subsequently resigned in November 1992 and the group changed its name to Signet Group in September 1993 because the Ratner brand had suffered immeasurably from this marketing faux pas.

It takes a lot of time and promotional work to establish yourself as an author and a brand name by following the tips set out in this book, but only a few minutes to lose that hard-won credibility and fan base by publishing books that have not been professionally proof read or making caustic remarks on discussion boards or on Amazon (as one best-selling e-book author did recently in criticising reviewers of his book, leading Amazon to throw him off the site for a period of time, costing him both readers and revenue).

As an author, you cannot separate yourself from your books completely even if you use a pen-name, because you still have to work with people who will be aware of the author's real name. In fact, writing under a pen-name can limit your marketing activities in some ways. Likewise, uploading positive reviews of your book disguised as 'anonymous' postings on discussion boards or adding five-star reviews of your book on Amazon can detract rather than enhance your book's marketing reach because it's obvious which glowing, detailed reviews are written by authors, especially those that say 'a must-read' and 'I cannot wait for the author's next book.'

If you criticise your publisher for not doing more, or harass retailers for not stocking your book, then no one will want to work with you and your books won't have a chance. Likewise, if your readers take time to review your book, even negatively, you should consider carefully what they say and respond positively to them. Take care not to take your readers for granted, or you will lose them more quickly than you gained them. Listen closely to your readers, and give them what they're asking for.

You and your books are your brand. Your books are your logo and will be your readers' first impression of you, hence it is vital that you get the title and the covers right. Along with the story-lines that you skilfully and painstakingly weave together, your author brand is how you pitch your work and how you conduct yourself.

Good examples of branding in the literary world are Mills and Boon. Everyone knows that they publish romantic novels. Stephen King is a horror and thriller writer that most people will know, which is why his name is larger than the title on his last five books. Julia Donaldson is author of over 120 children's books and on the cover of many of them it states boldly 'by the Children's Laureate and author of *The Gruffalo*'.

I took my children to see Julia Donaldson speak at the Wonderlands Festival of Writing at the British Library and expected a question-and-answer session with the author talking about herself, her main inspiration for writing best-loved children's stories, and what she's working on next. Instead, she involved most all of the hundred or so children in the audience over the course of an hour and acted out her stories and sang songs accompanied by her mulit-talented guitar-playing husband, Malcolm.

J. K. Rowling has set a great example to writers by playing down her success and being pragmatic during interviews. Many people will know that she wrote her early novels in cafes in Edinburgh because the walk there helped get her young daughter to sleep and that she was a single mother at the time. Her brand is her Harry Potter novels first, and her personal 'rags to riches' life story has added to her overall brand because she came from humble beginnings and downplays her success.

You are your brand. Get people to like you and they will want to read your books.

1

Production Tips
for Selling e-books

There are three key stages to publishing your book – production, pricing and promotion. The production of your book is as important as the storyline. If your book is already completed, then think about the content as you read this section. If you are currently writing it, then try to apply some of the following production tips which will give you hooks into potential sales pockets.

1   Write hooks into your e-book

When I began my first novel, *Soft Target*, to my mind it was a commercial entity. Yes, it was a thriller novel but I wanted to link in as many marketable hooks as I could to use at a later date. I knew that my goal was to manufacture a series so that the first book would sell further books, and vice-versa.

When marketing your books, start local, move to regional, national and eventually international markets. I wanted to concentrate my initial marketing in my locality to minimise travel expenses later. Hence all my books are set in and around Liverpool and the North West. If you can build a fan base in a big city, then you are on to a winner. Remember that word of mouth will sell more books than any other medium. If a fan of your novels tells their family and friends that a local landmark or street name, river, cathedral or train station is in the story then they can visualise the book as it progresses. It also gives you a hook into the local media which is really important.

Over the years, I have built a very personal relationship with journalists, editors, radio DJs and their associates, which is priceless when I have a new book or a book signing coming up. Remember that I didn't have a publisher behind me to pay for my books to be 'front of shop' in bookstores, or to make phone calls to reviewers to open doors. I had to knock on them myself.

An important point to remember is that unless you're a celebrity your book is not big news. Don't be disappointed if your local television station does not call you back or your local newspaper leaves you on hold until you finally hang up. I have had more doors slammed in my face than I can remember but as your sales grow, then so does the news value. When I launched my first book, nobody wanted to know and that is why you have to start on the bottom rung and take one step up the literary ladder at a time, working hard at building interest in you as a brand. Writing hooks into your books helps to achieve this.

2 Mention real places in your book

If you have any links to large organisations, then use them in the book. At the end of *Soft Target*, the local football derby is targeted by terrorists. Liverpool is a city full of football fans, blue and red. I am talking about millions of fans. Using the clubs in my book gave me a hook into the corporate side of the clubs and they invited me to do book signings at their pre-match corporate dinners. I also incorporated a scuba diving centre in the Lake District, which has thousands of members. They distributed bookmarks and sent e-mails to their members. These tips are case specific but the key point is to think about the content of your book and look for the hooks which can get your foot in the door. Use the places in your book to help you reach pockets of interest.

3 Use real names to build reader loyalty

Most of my books have the names of friends, family and more recently some of my readers in them. I use their first or second names usually because they have asked me to put them into the storyline. If you want someone to tell everyone that they meet about your book, put them in it. Be careful not to associate their character with their names but if done correctly, this generates word of mouth and builds sales. For instance, my brother is called Stanley Timothy Jones. I use a major in the terrorist taskforce named Stanley Timms. Another example is Sylvia Blythe, a detective in *The Child Taker*. The name is the maiden name of one of my biggest fans who also writes reviews for every novel. If you can build that kind of loyalty from readers then you will sell books to the people they talk to and good reviews are priceless. You will be amazed at how many of your friends and family promise to put a review on Amazon and never get around to it.

4 Keep your vocabulary simple and concise

You can write a masterpiece that is worthy of literary accolades and awards the world over but if it does not speak to your target audience then you are wasting your time creating it in the first place. Be careful to keep your story flowing and the language understandable. Have you seen the Kindle apps which explain the meaning of a word to you? If I have to look up more than one word in a chapter then the writer has already lost my interest. A classic example of this is the Bourne series. The films are non-stop action and ultra-exciting but the books are difficult to read and the vocabulary is complicated. Keep it simple; the storyline is more important to the reader than your knowledge of vocabulary.

5 Write an exciting first line, paragraph and chapter

Hit the ground running. You need to grab the attention of your reader in the first paragraph so they'll want to read more. If you look at your story objectively and don't believe that the first chapter excites or intrigues the reader, then change it or create a prologue which does. I have met dozens of readers at book signings who like my books because they start on page one rather than page fifty-one. Hook them on the first page and make sure that they stay hooked throughout the book.

6 Keep the story flowing – don't be over-descriptive

Don't get too wordy. With e-books you can provide a good amount of information in a succinct way. Resist the urge to tell too many stories unless they are specifically pertinent to the product or service that you are selling and *only* if they are applicable to the target audience. Descriptions of characters and places are important but keep the storyline flowing. Pace and plot are vital.

7 Use an e-book template, and add a 'Look Inside'

An e-book template will help you format the book as you write. E-book readers and apps are progressing and the quality is improving every year. Make sure that when the reader opens your novel that it looks as though it has come from a top flight publishing house. Most readers will check out the 'look inside this book' option which Amazon offers.

Make sure your book looks as if it's been put together by a publishing professional. Include a proper title page. Check your formatting hasn't gone awry during the conversion process, leaving gaps and different font sizes where they shouldn't be. This is a common occurrence when uploading large documents. White spaces such as paragraph spaces or any use of the space bar in the document can transform them into 'hard returns', so that sentences stop halfway across a line and continue on the next line down. This can lead to gaps in the novel which look unprofessional and can put off the reader.

8   Reflect the genre and content in the book title

The title is important to book buyers and new readers. Make sure the title of the book is descriptive of both the genre and content of the book. It's no good writing a crime thriller called *Love and Transformation*. The title might mean a lot to you as the author but it will probably mean nothing to a reader browsing the charts. One reason for the commercial success of *The Child Taker* is because the name attracts the massive female readers' market.

9   Judge your book by its cover

People often do judge a book by the cover. The cover is the first thing your book will be judged on. If your cover isn't eye-catching, particularly as a thumbnail, the reader or casual browser in a bookshop may pass it by without a second glance. The cover may look brilliant when it is full size but in the e-book world it will lose its detail if it is too busy. You will see many thumbnail covers that have been designed using Photoshop and they do stand out, but not for the right reasons. If your e-book isn't selling, why not try a new title or new cover?

My seventh novel was originally called *Slow Burn* and while it reached top ten in the Kindle charts it didn't sell as well as *The Child Taker* – yet my readers thought it was a better story. Readers' reviews told me the reason why. The cover depicts an Israeli flag burning, which readers associated with a terrorist-type novel. It is actually a tale of abuse, rape and revenge and is centred round a Jewish family, hence the flag.

I made a huge mistake with both the title and the cover and they are in the process of being changed, which is the beauty of e-books. You can fix things in a few hours.

10   Write a catchy back cover synopsis

Make sure you have a catchy synopsis and back cover blurb. Do not give the plotline away but hook the readers into reading your novel. If you've any reviews or celebrity endorsements then slot short, pithy quotes from them onto the back cover.

You can also edit your product description to incorporate any new five-star reviews that you receive and keep it updated. The first thing a reader will do is read the book's summary and reviews, especially the poor ones. Make the blurb concise and exciting. I read many blurbs that start with 'This is a story about...' and within a few sentences, they have lost the reader. Read some blurbs from best-selling novels in your genre and copy their style. There is nothing wrong with following another publishers' format.

11   Create an interesting preview

There are several ways to create a quick preview. If we mention websites that you are unfamiliar with, then go and have a quick look at them as we progress. Most of them will take less than fifteen minutes to have a virtual walk around so that you get the ideas that we're mentioning.

✦ Post screenshots (as images) of relevant pages alongside the initial index and content pages.

✦ Post relevant pages of your book alongside the initial index and content pages as html. This would also be a search engine optimised (SEO) way of promoting your e-book.

✦ You can use a Scribd (*www.scribd.com*) to publish and post a preview.

✦ You can create a Digital Flip Publication on CreateMagazines itself to publish and post a preview.

✦ Smashwords (*www.smashwords.com*) has a good guide on formatting which is free to download.

12   Build a relationship with your readers

Use your e-book as the start of building a relationship with your readers. This is not the last time you will help or entertain them, but the first time. You only get one chance to make a first impression, so if you intend to write several books then it is important to get the first one right. One of the great things about the e-book market is that readers can get a quick and immediate fix and when they've read something of yours that they've enjoyed, they can easily buy something else at just the click of a button.

A collection of short stories at a low price is a great way to introduce readers to your style. Moreover, it doesn't cost much to have a short collection edited and doesn't take the best part of a year to write. Short stories will increase your virtual shelf-space and make you more noticeable to the reader. When I published *Nine Angels* it was a short story written in a month, but it flew up the horror charts because of the readership that I had already established.

13   Choose your digital platform carefully

It is very important to select the right e-book. Amazon's KDP (Kindle digital platform) is the big boy on the block and it has several key factors that you should consider before you upload your e-book to multiple sites. If you choose KDP and enrol in the Kindle prime programme, then you can offer your book free to readers for five days in every ninety-day period. Believe me when I tell you that offering your book for free opens it up to thousands and thousands of new readers. If you have multiple novels or are writing a series, then it is essential.

Last time I offered *The Child Taker* free for five days, over 12,000 people downloaded it. It climbed to number 2 in the Kindle free charts and when the price went back to normal, it re-entered the normal charts at number thirteen and earned me £800 over the next two days.

If you choose Kindle then you have to make your book exclusive to them. There are good alternatives. A publishing platform like Zinepal (*www.zinepal.com*) creates your PDF e-book in a format that most common e-book readers can display, allowing you the virtue of uploading your e-book to multiple sites.

14   Sell through multiple e-bookstores/directories

Although top e-book stores like Amazon, Barnes & Noble and Apple account for the bulk of e-book sales, there are several smaller but equally important e-book stores which could boost your e-book sales substantially including KOBO (*www.kobobooks.com*), Books On Board (*www.booksonboard.com*), Diesel book store, and so on.

Another way to maximise sales for your e-book is to take advantage of e-book directories that accept direct submissions from authors. While most major e-book sellers like Amazon or Barnes & Noble only accept submissions from major book publishers, many of the smaller online e-book retailers or 'e-tailers' will accept e-book submissions from writers. Smashwords can get your book into the big chains, if you follow their formatting policies.

15 Create a sales page optimised for search engines

When you are selling an e-book you are offering it via the internet. So it makes sense to have a dedicated page for your e-book which sets out everything that your potential readers would want to know and thus lead to a sale. You can use this webpage to provide author information, book information or introduce special offers and have your own e-commerce system in place to sell your e-book right from your own webpage. This way you would not be sharing profits with anyone else.

When you offer your e-book for sale from e-book stores you generally end up receiving between 30% and 70% of your gross sales figures. The remaining amount is kept by the e-book stores as their cut. Though offering your e-book through e-book stores is an absolute necessity as these stores are able to provide substantial exposure to your e-book, why not have your own sales page in place too? You can either create a simple webpage on your own, or hire a company to create one for you.

16 Make the book available in multiple file formats

Different users have different reading preferences. Some like to read their e-books on a personal computer, some on an e-book reader device like Kindle or Nook, some like to read them on new Tablet devices like iPad and some like to read them on their mobile devices. The problem is that each one of these devices has its own set of compatible file formats. So it makes good sense to have your e-book in multiple file formats so that you have an extended reach and are able to provide a format compatible with several of these popular devices. Calibre is a free download program that converts your word document into e-book format accepted by most e-readers.

17 *Use E-Junkie for e-book delivery and affiliates*

E-Junkie ties into PayPal (and other payment providers) and currently costs about £3 a month.

2

Pricing Tips

How much an author should charge for their e-book is a difficult dilemma. When you think of how many hours were spent on its creation, then even working on the minimum wage it should be worth thousands! After the editing, formatting and cover art has been checked, we need to look carefully at what is the best price that will probably generate the most sales. This is a question which will baffle every publisher or aspiring e-book author before they take the brave step into the wild digital-jungles of the e-book revolution.

18   Price your e-book intelligently

Pricing has always been a contentious issue. Many indie authors have seen success because they've been able to undercut the big boys. However, the 99p price tag may lose some of its allure unless readers know that they are buying quality. Short stories involving the characters from your novel can be offered for a low price or free in order to drum up interest in your novels.

19   Avoid under-pricing your book

A good price for novels is £2.99, novellas and a short story for £1.99 or 99p. As the market grows and readers switch from tree-books to e-books the expectation of quality grows too. I have often heard readers comment that the 99p bracket belongs to self-published authors. Although I don't necessarily agree with that, it is important to listen to general opinion and react accordingly.

20 Set a low price point for your first book

If you have multiple titles, a low price may hook people in to buying your others at a higher price.

21 Experiment with pricing and monitor closely

Never be afraid to run promotions and drop the price to entice new readers. You can change the price with the click of a button.

If you are planning a launch and it is your first book, be careful not to undervalue it in the early weeks. Pick a realistic price point and stick to it for the allotted duration of the launch. If it is a new addition to your series of books, set the price slightly higher than the already published catalogue as there will be readers waiting to buy it and they will not mind paying a fair price for your new works.

Ultimately the price of the e-book is a crucial decision which only you can make. The hard and fast rule of the traditional book stores does not apply here and some unorthodox approaches are allowed, so experiment until you find the happy medium which leads to success.

The digital world is an instant one and setting the right price is a fluid entity. If you realise that your book and the weight that it carries will change over time and may fluctuate with performance, then it will take the pressure off this issue to 'get it right'. If you are not happy with it, then you can change it. A new book may at first seem outlandishly priced at £6.99 but after six months of constantly being in the top tier, can easily become a bargain!

Public perception will change as your sales increase whether it is 99p or £2.99. However, many successful authors are convinced that the 99p pricing bracket is the most successful. Remember that the most downloaded books on sale are dwarfed by the number of free e-books available.

Trying to play safe and stick to the status quo on pricing is a good bet but being optimistic and placing more value in your work is not a bad thing either. Try it, evaluate it and react to the results you see over a reasonable period of time. The mainstream e-book community may not legitimise an overly-optimistic approach but every marketing campaign involves some measure of trial and error, especially when it comes to pricing for digital downloads. If the higher price point doesn't work, you can readily change it, but only do so after a period of marketing and analysis of the results.

There is a perception that the huge number of e-books being produced will dilute the amount of readers you can reach. This is nonsense. Try not to feed into the illusion of being swamped by the competition. There are far more quality e-books being read now than ever before. Furthermore, the projection from Amazon, Apple, Smashwords and Forbes is that e-book consumers are set to spend between £2 and £3 *billion* on e-books in 2013, rising to a staggering £6 *billion* in 2016.

22   Charge what you would pay for the book

There is no firm and fast golden rule to e-book pricing but the key factor to consider is that an author must charge what they believe, objectively, that they themselves would pay for it. Being critical here is key, and attempting to step out of oneself and become the potential buyer should help you pick the ideal price point. You have to be realistic. If you are, then why should anyone believe an e-book is worth more or less than what the author thinks?

Remember that the content rules supreme. How many stories did ancient Egyptian scribes write down? No one knows for sure, but very few written on papyrus scrolls have survived the centuries since their creation, and how much would historians pay to have those few stories? They would be priceless because of the value they place on them.

23   Base pricing on quality, not on book length

The length of the e-book is not as important as the content within it. The quality is what adds value, and providing a great product of some sort for the reader will dictate the value. One should never think in terms of how many words there are when pricing an e-book.

Digital downloads are far different from printed books in that generally there is a direct correspondence between page count and print costs which determine the recommended retail prices for print copies. Yet with e-books, there are no production costs to factor into the pricing structure, and thus the 'value' is based solely on quality, not quantity. This is the main reason that e-book pricing is so fluid rather than fixed, as is the case with printed versions, and why it involves careful deliberation and monitoring.

The pricing of your e-book is an important decision, and one which you can change, but once you have decided on a price it should be adhered to for a decent period of time. Changing the price every other day looks bad and may annoy readers. Use promotions, be confident and realistic and stick with your gut instinct. The readers will soon let you know if you have got it wrong.

3
Promotional Tips – Online

When you are preparing your marketing plans, timing is crucial. If you are looking for a magic formula to sell 10,000 copies of your book, then you'll be disappointed. There is no one solution. You have to use the shotgun method, during which you are aiming multiple activities at the same target. Whether you are about to launch or relaunch your book, you have to spend some time planning all your promotional activities and making sure that you coordinate them for maximum effect.

24   Keep a checklist of promotional activity

Build up interest in your launch weeks before the actual date but make sure that your book is uploaded and available prior to the launch. Don't waste a media opportunity by announcing in July that your book will be available from next Christmas because unless you are already a household name, no one will remember.

You need to set up a checklist where you can record your activities, set completed-by dates and tick each activity off when it's accomplished. Never throw the checklist away as you can use it for reference in years to come. Keep as much detail as you can until you have experimented with the format that works for you. For example:

Activity	When	Completed	Comments/results
Send out bookmarks to local readers' group Birchwood Readers c/o 44 Holly Drive WA4 6YU Appleton Book Club c/o 42 Willis Rd WA5 4QZ	One week before launch	Yes	Received invitation to present at their March meeting. Contact Dave Mann 07768957687
Contact Susan at Radio Merseyside 0151-487-0000 susan@bbc.radio	One week after launch	Called Tuesday	Appearing on Susan's show 5/2/2012
Send letters to colleges in North Wales	Two months before launch	Sent out twenty-three letters	Had fifteen replies and two invites to present in March

I used a daily, weekly, monthly and six-monthly to-do list to keep me organised. For example:

Daily	Weekly	Monthly	Six-monthly
Check sales reports			
Record any comments on highs and lows	Send out batch of twenty letters	Update contact lists	Update local radio
Check book reviews and reply to the reviewer	Send out bookmarks	Update marketing plan	Update local TV
Check Facebook and update status. Reply to any messages	Update book reviews on Goodreads	Update local newspaper	

As a writer, it's all too easy to become totally engrossed in writing your next book and thus neglect your marketing plan, which is paramount to the commercial success of your book. And until you are disciplined enough to follow a monthly routine automatically use a 'to-do' list daily.

25 *Do not spend any money on advertising*

Avoid engaging companies to draft or distribute press releases for you. I published *Soft Target* as a paperback with one of the biggest international self-publishing companies around. They offered some marketing packages, which on paper looked amazing but in reality I spent £3,000 that I couldn't afford without seeing any tangible return on my investment.

You will be keen and enthusiastic about getting your message to as many people as possible and paying someone to do it for you appears to be the easy option but I guarantee that you will waste your money, especially if you are an independent author. Most blanket press releases don't make it past the spam filters and as we said before, your book is not news yet.

I paid a small fortune to my publishers and they promised to distribute press releases to newspapers and radio stations all across the USA and UK. That was in 2008 and I'm still waiting for the phone to ring from the media sources confirming receipt of the press release and requesting an interview. Don't waste your money; you will have to do this yourself.

Similarly, I met a self-published thriller writer who had a personal friend working in the advertising department at a glossy men's monthly magazine. It is a well-established publication with a huge readership. His friend secured him a double-page spread advertising his book for free. It sounded like an author's dream come true; two glossy pages to advertise your book with an editorial about the author and the plot. I was insanely jealous and could not wait to see the results of such a press campaign. He ordered hundreds of hard copies of his novel in anticipation of the sales rush for his books. All his internet sellers were stocked up and ready to go and his e-book was uploaded and polished to perfection.

When the magazine came out, he logged online every hour on the hour to check sales. Nothing happened, and in fact he sold fewer copies that month than in the month before. The advertising space would have cost him thousands. He was devastated by the result but if he had bought that advert, I think he would have bitterly regretted it.

26   Seek out third-party endorsements

Use the power of social media to spread the word about your e-book. The internet is the key to letting an unknown author place their novel next to the biggest names in the literary world. If you use it correctly, you can generate a lot of interest in your books. If you get it wrong, you will become an annoying internet troll harassing everyone. It is a fine line, so do be careful. Be polite at all times even when people criticise your work. Remain positive and friendly or you will lose readers when you are trying to gain them and endear people to you as the author.

Social media marketing (also known as SMO) has become a popular tool to promote just about everything that you can possibly think of. Sites like Twitter, Facebook, YouTube, LinkedIn, Ning, Bebo and blogs and vBlogs all allow authors to 'repost' or share information about themselves and their e-book easily. Since the same information is shared by a reader with their contacts and hopefully by contacts of their contact, it helps in spreading the word fast, thus reaching more and more potential readers.

Remember that bad news travels faster than good so be careful when interacting with readers. I have witnessed some long-winded exchanges on book review sites which would make you cringe. Eventually the argument becomes the focus rather than the book or the review. Social networking sites act as word of mouse (viral) promotion adding more value to your book, so do not underestimate the damage you could do by being obtuse. Third-party endorsements are the best recommendation that you can hope for and readers love it when you comment on their review of your book, even if it is a poor review. Remember that they have spent their money buying your book, invested their time in reading it and then taken the time to sit down and write a review. They are entitled to their opinion.

A social network facilitates regular communication between individuals who are connected by friendship or common interest. Most common interest manifests itself as a group. All you have to do is search keywords linked to your book and you will find groups to join. You can use these networks to enhance your personal network, and grow sales. The key is to use all appropriate functions of a given social network for maximum benefit.

Facebook (*www.facebook.com*) allows you to create a profile, join groups of people with similar interests, discuss your personal interests, and communicate with friends and potential customers. Facebook is massive and is a gift to the unknown author. Every author should be on Facebook.

If you already have a Facebook page then hopefully you have established the basics. Go to the 'search friend' space at the top of your profile and type in 'Kindle'. Over twenty groups will appear and you need to join all of them. Some of them will be invitation only but you can request an invite.

27 Build your profession into your Facebook name

My Facebook name is 'Conrad Jones, bestselling Kindle author'. That is not for vanity; it's because I want people to know that they have found the right Conrad Jones. When I ask to join a writing group, it is obvious that I have something to offer the group.

28 Build your profile positively

When you have joined a group, make sure that you interact in a positive manner and add the other members as friends. This way your profile as a writer is growing and you are reaching dozens and dozens of people who are interested in books. Do not just join and post a link to your Amazon page and then disappear or you will turn people off you very quickly. Joining a group for shameless self-promotion will not gain you any fans; in fact, it's likely to have the opposite effect.

29 Join relevant online groups

Using the search bar, type in 'authors' and 'writers' and dozens of groups will appear. Join them and follow the steps above. Add their members to your friends list and remember that the more friends you have and the more interesting your posts are, the more people will be interested in you and your books. Just introduce yourself to the group and express the desire to talk to other authors and readers about writing and promoting books. Mention that you are looking for reviewers to give you feedback. Don't forget to send speedy replies to any communication you receive.

30 Update and inform readers about your books

Once again, search. Type in 'readers' this time, but you must be careful with readers' sites. Readers' sites detest self-promotion, especially from unknown self-published authors. I know from experience they can be easily offended. Join as many groups as possible and add as many friends from those groups as you can and then dedicate time every day to update and inform people about your books and launch dates by updating your profile status.

31   Increase your friends/contacts and set up an event

This will be the launch of your e-book. Make sure you set up a Twitter (*www.twitter.com*) account and a LinkedIn (*www.linkedin.com*) site before you set up your event as they all link through the same page on Facebook. Once again, if you aren't familiar with these sites, then take ten minutes to look at them and familiarise yourself with how they work. It will probably take you fifteen minutes to half an hour to set yourself up with a profile when you are ready to.

32   Keep your author page fun and interesting

Set up your author page on Amazon by going to the Author Central page, and link it to your Twitter and Facebook pages. All you do is click on the icons and the software does the rest for you. Along with your blog, these three sites are crucial to any internet campaign. Build your profiles with pictures, book covers and reviews. Keep it fun and interesting and people will be regular visitors to your site.

If you are getting ready to publish a book then you have to 'get up to speed' with social media marketing. A lot of authors I talk to want to learn about social media and how it's going to help them sell thousands of books but they hesitate, because they're not confident with it. They know they need to be building their author platform and brand, but don't know how Twitter fits in. It's a simple platform to send regular updates and build an audience. There are only a few things you can actually do on Twitter but simple is good. Everything else that flows from your involvement with it comes from the network of people you connect with.

It takes time and effort to build a following. If you have no followers then you are wasting your time. You have to grow a community around the value of the content and ideas you share on the site.

33 Add 'author' or 'writer' to your Twitter username

On Twitter, make sure your username name is not random or too long; ten or twelve characters should do. Remember that your username on Twitter needs to include 'author' or 'writer' in it if you're going to use it for promoting your book. It is part of your branding strategy.

34 Use Twitterific

There is free software that makes Twitter a lot easier to use. Twitterific on the iPad and the iPhone are good, though there are many others so it's worth looking around to see what works for you. The software allows you to automate your Twitter profile which saves time.

Being able to schedule Tweets in advance is a big advantage and you can auto-tweet, which gives you the ability to plan a campaign.

Here are some pointers for using Twitter.

+ Don't read *every* tweet.

+ Follow anyone who follows you (and unfollow spammers).

+ Promote other people twelve times to every one self-promotional tweet.

+ Build lists to watch people who matter to you more closely.

+ Retweet the good stuff from others. Sharing is caring.

✦ A lot of @replies shows a lot of humanity and engagement.

✦ Robot tweets are less effective than human tweets.

✦ Promote the new/less followed authors more than the well-established 'names'.

✦ Set an egg timer. Twitter is addictive.

✦ Everyone tweets in their own way. You're doing it wrong, too – to someone.

The same principles that apply to social media apply to social networking in general, especially when building up a group of readers who are keen to hear about your publishing plans.

35 Search out relevant contacts in the book world

Target your searches to find the people with the biggest followings in your genre. Once you find them, you can start looking through the list of who they are following to find more people to follow. Build up your followers, which takes time, hence my advice on planning a launch well in advance. Even if you have already launched, set up your profile and spend time regularly building followers.

36 Search the list pages

Search for e-books review groups and e-book retweeting groups of which there are many. Some will have over 100,000 followers so if they pick up one of your promotional tweets and pass it on, the results are incredible. There are many writers and publishers who you can follow for great information and tips. Try to find lists created by experts in your field and retweet any useful links to your followers.

37 Keep an eye on followers

If we assume that you are now following important people in your niche, you should check them out on a daily basis. Remember to keep adding followers too. Keep your focus tight at first so you don't overwhelm yourself with input. Read the tweets from these industry leaders and add the people with lots of followers. Click through anything that looks interesting to see what they are linking to. Watch especially for links that get retweeted or passed along.

38   Tweet useful links and ideas

There's no rush. I read tweets for two or three months before I sent out any tweets of my own. Be patient and keep watching and soon you'll see why some people are popular and lots of people want to follow them. It is usually because they consistently provide links and ideas that are valuable; or because they make an effort to connect with people individually.

39   Pick up followers with useful content

Once you've worked out what's considered valuable in the communities you're following, it's time to become a participant. Do a little searching and see if you can find resources that have not been mentioned recently and pass it on. If you use your Facebook account to post links then it will automatically send it to Twitter and LinkedIn. Create a short tweet alerting people to this resource, put in a shortened link and tweet it.

40   Retweet other authors

Retweeting builds brand loyalty. This is all about sharing discoveries, sharing content and not about direct selling. You are building trust and a trusted community of followers; at the same time you are receiving valuable tips from the people you are following.

41   Build trust with your tweets

Be polite to all even when abuse is tweeted in your direction. There are thousands of trolls out there with nothing better to do than annoy people on the internet. If you encounter them, be professional. You will gain the respect of the rest of the community if you handle yourself with dignity. Remember that others can see your conversations unless they are private messages. Abusive arguments in clear view of the community will alienate your readers.

In essence, you are asking people who you have never met to trust you and read your e-book. This is done most effectively by adding value to others and not by tweeting anything you have not personally verified yourself. Trust is the most important element in the community you are building.

42   Use postings links and photographs

Twitter is truly an amazing phenomenon, considering it only consists of 140 characters of basic text. Become familiar with posting links and photographs. They will create interest in you and your book. The creativity, the energy and vitality on Twitter is astonishing. It can be a great place to connect to people who are interested in your work, and who in turn will send your message out into their own networks of followers.

43   Join LinkedIn

Follow the same rules as for the Facebook tips. Remember that LinkedIn is a professional site for executives and senior management from every industry. There is a multitude of author groups, publishers groups, self-publishers, agents and marketing forums. The site gives you the facility to invite everyone in your email address list to join your network by simply clicking one button. The author groups and marketing forums are extremely vibrant and useful.

44 Join marketing groups and book forums

Set aside half an hour every day to participate in the forums. Read the discussions in the marketing forums as there are hundreds of people asking the same questions as you. There is a plethora of information to be learned on this site and people are very quick to point out any pitfalls that they have fallen into. Learning from other authors' mistakes is a valuable exercise.

45 Link your LinkedIn account to other accounts

Twitter and Facebook accounts will synchronise at the click of an icon, which saves you a lot of time and effort. These channels thrive on authentic social interactions, so be careful not to overtly sell yourself or your e-book to avoid alienating the connections you make. For example, rather than posting multiple messages about your e-book being available for sale, try to contribute meaningful dialogue in conversations about relevant and related topics. This will position you as an intelligent writer, which will help to build your author brand.

Be careful not to hassle agents and publishers. I have seen some cringe-worthy conversations between disparaging, know-it-all writers and not-so desperate agents. They tend to be short, one-sided affairs with abrupt endings!

Talk about your e-book in an open forum intelligently and realistically. Don't claim to have sold ten thousand copies of your e-book when your Amazon ranking proves that you have sold ten. You can share any genuine reviews that you receive and post links to your e-book, which gives your target audience the chance to glance at your work and make up their own minds about its merits.

LinkedIn is a useful tool for making business connections and meeting other authors, but remember that it is just another tool in the box. Even the most active users miss on some simple ways to optimise the way they use LinkedIn. Below are a few more tips on how to make the most of your LinkedIn presence.

✦ Think about your goals. Why are you on LinkedIn? Is it to find new readers and other authors? To be found? Some mix of the two? Your goals should drive your entire presence on the site.

✦ Post a picture of your face. You should have a professional-looking headshot as your LinkedIn photo so people can put a name to a face. If you're uncomfortable with readers or prospective agents seeing your picture next to your professional credentials (a valid concern), you can change your privacy settings so only your connections can see your photo.

✦ Use LinkedIn to help remember names. LinkedIn can help you with offline networking too. Simply checking on someone's profile after meeting them at a networking event, even if you don't connect, can help you remember their name and what they do. This is another reason why having a picture is important – it will help people remember you.

✦ Make the most of your LinkedIn headline. Your headline does not have to be your job title alone. Keep it concise, but make sure that it conveys what you do and what your skills are.

✦ Post status. Updating your status gives you visibility on your connections' LinkedIn home page. If you have found something online you think your business connections would like, or you have good news to share about your work, spread the word by posting it on LinkedIn.

✦ Write a content-rich but concise summary. Your summary should be about you, not your book. Use concrete details like results you have generated and the work you do on a daily basis to show people how professional you are.

✦ Explore various LinkedIn applications. Add Amazon's Reading List application to your LinkedIn profiles. If you are not sure how the fiction you read is relevant to your professional connections, think again. I get more comments on this list than anything else in my profile.

✦ Add sections to your profile. LinkedIn offers several sections beyond the standards so users can showcase their volunteer experience, projects, foreign languages, even test scores. This is especially helpful for new networkers who may not have extensive work experience outside of writing a book. Adding more sections can add weight to any profile.

✦ Connect with care. Your network is only as valuable as the strength of your connections. For some professionals, it is advantageous to connect generally, but I tend to favour smaller useful lists. If you would like to connect with someone and think it might be a stretch, be sure to personalise the message you send with the invite to explain why you want to connect and why this person should want to connect with you.

✦ Join and participate in discussion groups. Some groups are full of spam, drivel and dross, but others are generally valuable. For example, in the book marketing groups there are great places to get and give free advice. Do a little research, think back to your goals, and you'll probably find groups that will help you reach them. If you can't find a group, just start one!

46 Join MySpace, Ning, Bebo and video-sharing sites

There are many similar general-interest networks and video sharing websites like YouTube which are essential as you progress. Each has different functions and advantages. YouTube is ideal for posting book trailers, linking to any footage of television appearances or advertising clips you produce yourself promoting your e-book.

47 Put your protagonist on Facebook and Twitter

If you're planning a series of books with a serial protagonist, try creating a Facebook or Twitter account for your protagonist and hold conversations in the voice of that character. The Jack Reacher (Lee Child) forums are constantly busy with readers and avid fans discussing the fictional hero as if he's real. It is not everyone's cup of tea but it works for several authors.

48 Join social networks

There are networks designed to connect business professionals such as Plaxo, Ryze and most recently BranchOut (a Facebook/LinkedIn hybrid). You can target some networks based on the content of your book. Follow the steps for your Facebook profile. The sites are linked so you might as well take full advantage of the exposure they can offer.

49 Join social bookmarking sites

Link with as many other authors as you can. To communicate with other authors and avid readers, try Shelfari or weRead where you can rate, review, and discuss your book, as well as books by other authors. Use Meetup to find and join groups united by a common interest such as politics, books, games, movies, careers or hobbies. Sites like Digg, Pinterest, Delicious, StumbleUpon, Buzzfeed, Slashdot and Reddit are social bookmarking services for storing, sharing and discovering popular content. Find and use the best ones for your book.

50 Connect with vendors and marketers

Affiliate programs offered by sites like ClickBank and Tradebit can also help you to market your e-book as they provide online marketplaces for digital information products. The sites aim to serve as a connection between digital content creators (known as 'vendors') and affiliate marketers, who then promote the relevant content to consumers.

51 Avoid pay-per-click

Don't spend much on Google adwords and other 'pay-per-click' traffic generators. I have seen campaigns run by authors who have a lot more marketing money than most fall flat on their face. Remember that free advertising is the best way to raise your literary profile and build up a readership for your e-book.

52 Write a blog and keep it current

You need a good blog because people want 'conversation' about the topic of your e-book. It will also help you with Google ratings. A blog builds relationships and credibility. I tend to use Facebook for short daily updates as they are shared automatically with my other sites and then if people are interested in my posts, they will interact. This is a great way for building up links with both readers and writers. You can use your blog to build your platform, exposure, and credibility as an expert on your topic. Keep it authentic, post to it regularly and respond to visitor comments quickly and professionally.

If you cannot commit to writing a regular blog, consider creating occasional content for other blogs which pertain to the topic of your book. Reach out to similar bloggers for guest blog opportunities, and invite them to be a guest on your blog. To get started blogging, consider using a template provided by services like Wordpress, and feature your blog on your website.

Some authors find video blogs (or vBlogs) useful in selling their e-books. There are three main components.

The first is vBlog software. There are a number of options in this regard. Blogger is commonly used by many as it is a free and hosted service, but to make Blogger work you'll have to know or learn some basic computer programming (HTML). Alternatively, if you're willing to pay a nominal fee, you can try TypePad which has more features and is easier to use.

The second component is another hosted service called vBlog Central which hosts photos and videos, automatically converts the videos into Windows, QuickTime, and Real formats, and can automatically link them to your blog.

The third part is actually creating the video itself, preferably with a digital video camcorder with professional editing functionality so that you can ensure your video is the best it can be.

53   Promote your book professionally

Remember, whatever promotional material you decide to release in support of your e-book will be a reflection on your e-book. If you produce an unedited, unprofessional Youtube video or vBlog to showcase your book, it can put readers off. If you own a shop and have an amateurish-looking shop window display, it's not going to draw people in. Your promotion should be as professional as your book display.

54   Seek reviews and reply to all of them

Get your e-books reviewed by as many friends and family members as you can. Books with published reviews and real testimonials from various e-book stores or your readers tend to get more attention and interest and thus sell more. I try to reply to every review, good or bad. If it is good then you can build a rapport with the reviewer, which tends to generate more positive reviews from them in the future.

If they are scathing then either ignore it, or be polite and thank them for the time they spent reading your book. I have seen hilarious discussion threads between wounded authors and reviewers. Some of them are very heated and almost abusive, but at the end of the day their opinion is just that, their opinion. You cannot change that.

One best-selling thriller writer was banned from Amazon recently because of his constant battles with and criticism of negative reviewers. The long-term result was that the author turned hundreds, if not thousands of potential readers, off his books. As mentioned earlier, your brand is both you and the book. If they don't like you, then they won't buy, endorse or recommend your books; it's as simple as that.

55   Offer limited period discounts and create bundles

Just like any e-commerce product, an e-book can be offered at a reduced rate for a short time or combine with related products to increase the overall value or worth of the deal to the user.

56   Build a loyal readership

Plan to write a series of novels and let people know that there will be more to come. Listen to your readers and give them what they ask for. One main virtue of publishing e-books is you can turn them out much quicker than traditionally published books. And if you're adept enough to develop an avid fan base, you have the benefit of knowing exactly what they want next.

On a related note, communicate directly with your readers, and communicate with them often. Write back to each of the fans who have written to you over the years – keep all of their messages – to let them know about the book and your plans for your next book. Listen to your avid readers, keep them happy and they'll return to buy your books time and time again.

57   Offer the first chapter for free

Another marketing strategy is to give away the first chapter free on sites like Mass-Ebooks, but include a bold link and a call to action in the chapter telling people how to buy the rest of the e-book. Make sure that you do this for a limited period, as free or discounted offers for e-books that seem to go on and on can actually diminish your brand name.

4

Promotional Tips – Offline

This section explains how to build interest in yourself and your e-book in the real world as opposed to the virtual, using a small marketing budget.

58   Search local directories for relevant links

Search the internet and local directories to find groups and associations that might be interested in your e-book and the story behind its creation. Sit down and write a list of places and people that you associate your past with. It doesn't matter how tenuous the links are – write them down. Include where you went to school, colleges, university, chess clubs, scout groups, Irish dancing classes! It doesn't matter how brief your association was, write down everything that comes into your head. I found that people were proud that an ex-pupil, ex-member, ex-student has become a published author and the opportunities which come from contacting them in a professional manner, are endless. Many will invite you to speak to their current pupils, members etc and even if they don't, some of them will tell their families and friends who will buy your books out of curiosity.

59   Contact the local press

When I published my first book, I received coverage from the *Holyhead and Anglesey Mail* and *The North Wales Chronicle* which boasted how a local man was launching his first novel and that Holyhead was one of the settings in the book. There were multiple

links there because I was a Holyhead author and the port was integral
to the plot.

The same month, the *St Helens Reporter* carried a story about a local
author whose family went back generations in the town, launching his
first e-book. I was born there, so they claimed me as theirs! The
Chester Chronicle covered the story, as did the Warrington papers and
the Liverpool editions. The *Manchester Evening News* also published a
half-page article. I used the hook that I was loyal to that area and my
book was forged from the burglary which had rendered me
unemployed. It wasn't just a book launch written by an unknown, it
had become a human interest story.

Once they have published an article about you, they are keen for
updates. Be careful not to bother journalists too often. Keep your
updates limited to real news, such as reaching number ten in the
charts or releasing a new novel. The point is that three cities and
several large towns are now on my media list when I have a new novel
coming out. Nine times out of ten, they print updates when I contact
them.

My other hook was the IRA bombing of Warrington Bridge Street in
1993. I was an assistant manager at the Bridge Street McDonald's
when two bombs exploded just after midday. The explosions were
directly outside the store and two young boys died that day. Once we
evacuated the restaurant, some of us tried to administer first aid to the
bomb victims.

I was deeply affected by the events of that day and it sparked an
interest which became the basis to my writing years later. I read
anything that I could get my hands on about terrorists and criminal

gangs and their baneful motivations. *Soft Target* was inspired by the events of that day. My biography indicates where my inspiration came from and again, it is a powerful human interest angle from which a journalist can pitch a story.

When you are looking for hooks into your e-book, think about your life and how you can hook people into it.

60   Write personalised letters to local venues

I contacted my old schools by writing letters to their English departments and offered my time to talk to their pupils about writing and publishing books. I didn't pester anybody with e-mails or phone calls. I took the time to write detailed personal letters and then left it to them to contact me. In the world of technology that we live in, there is still nothing to match the impact of a well-written personalised letter.

61   Tailor presentations to book writing

I then contacted schools and colleges in all the towns that I mentioned in my e-book. Later when sales were building, I contacted Liverpool University and the Universities in Manchester and Chester and received the same response. My diary was beginning to fill up as I was invited to talk to groups.

I pitched my presentations along the lines of why and how I wrote the book rather than the storyline. That way I held the interest of readers and non-readers. All of a sudden my book sales began to rise even before I had actually appeared anywhere. It was obvious that teachers and their associates were buying my book out of interest and my fan base and readership was growing.

62 Seek out regional associations

The next stage was to step outside of the personal arena. I looked for anywhere that large groups gathered for meetings. I chose the Rotary Clubs to begin with. There are six around Warrington alone and over twenty in and around Liverpool. Once I had contacted them, I moved on to Chester, St Helens and North Wales areas. This association consists of men mostly over retirement age. They have plenty of time to read. Most of the chapters meet once a week and they invite speakers to their dinners. The majority of speakers are looking for donations from the Rotary Club for one cause or another, so a speaker with a human interest story was like a breath of fresh air to them. Soon my Rotary connections were inviting me to speak at joint dinner events which consist of the male organisation and the female members who are known as the Inner Wheel. Now the gatherings were reaching over fifty people, sometimes more, and my book sales were growing rapidly.

63 Contact writing groups

There are thousands of creative writing groups across the country and I targeted them too. A list of 200+ UK writing groups, along with e-mail contact details, are included in Appendix 3 at the end of this book. Be careful if you approach these groups. Draft an interesting letter of introduction and offer your time for free. You will get your expenses paid when they buy your books and tell their friends about you.

I had a mixed response from writing groups because I was self-published at the time. There are lots of people who don't class independent authors as credible authors. They think that if you couldn't find a publisher, then it is because your book is not good enough, when in fact there are many talented authors who never get a look-in with established literary agents or traditional publishers until and unless they're already well-known. It's a catch-22 which many authors know only all too well. J. K. Rowling received numerous rejections from publishers, not because her book was about a young boy named Harry Potter wasn't good enough, but because of publishers' reluctance to invest in unknown authors. Once you successfully build up your author platform, more publishers will seriously consider your work.

64 Contact local and regional libraries

There are thousands of reading groups, mostly based in libraries. I contacted all the council-run libraries in all the towns that I mentioned and received invites to speak from many but not all. When I had positive feedback from a reading group, the library would order copies of my books for the entire group to read. This applies to both e-books as well as tree-books. If I spoke to a library group, it usually lasted all night! They love asking questions and talking about writing and books. Be careful to schedule enough time to talk to these groups at your leisure so that you don't offend anyone by constantly checking your watch or rushing off.

In Appendix 4, you will find a list of library contacts for the English counties, Wales, Scotland and the London boroughs.

65 Leave a gift

Find out how many people are expected, leave a gift behind but never ask for any money in return. Remember that selling and marketing are two different entities. You are trying to build interest and loyalty in your brand name and a small inexpensive gift connected to your book will always be well-received. I searched online for bookmarks and postcards and found several sites where you can purchase quality products at a reasonable price; if you have a few hundred pounds to spare then that's fine; buy quality bookmarks. You can buy inexpensive postcards with your book cover printed on them from online printers.

I did not want to increase my overheads further as travelling and eating out was costly enough. I used my laptop to design bookmarks and bought thin sheets of card to print them on. If I was talking to a Rotary Club, then I would download their logo and put my book covers on one side and their logo on the reverse. I did the same with football clubs, libraries, schools and colleges. I bought a guillotine and cut the bookmarks neatly which was time-consuming but kept costs down. At every presentation that I did, I made sure that everyone received one and I left some for any members who hadn't been able to attend.

66 Ensure promotional materials are current

Make sure your contact details and your website and any other relevant book links are printed on any promotional material you use, and that the information is up to date. Some people wanted them signed which is great as you cannot sign an e-book!

67 Leave your Facebook and Twitter details

Wherever you go, make sure that people know that you can be found on Facebook and Twitter and leave your email address. I printed my profile details and web addresses on each bookmark. That way you will build a working contact list which you can use to promote your next book launch or book signing event. If you build a relationship with people, then they will be interested in what you are doing next.

68 Monitor sales closely

Another benefit of e-books is that you can see your sales and sales rankings on an hourly basis. Set yourself a time every day when you check and monitor your figures. The overnight sales tend to update at about ten o'clock the next morning. Hopefully you will see the sales spikes following your promotional activities. For instance, I found if I had an after dinner speaking engagement on a Thursday night, my books would climb up the rankings on Friday.

Always track your figures. You cannot react to sales decreases if you don't know that they are decreasing. Keep a record of what works and what doesn't work as it will save you time and effort later on. Don't waste your valuable time on individuals or groups who do not buy into your message. Move on and concentrate on the next gig.

Remember that as an author, you have to grow a thick skin. Not everyone will like you or your book and you'll become accustomed to people hanging up the telephone or being patronising and condescending. Take it on the chin; it's not personal and you will probably never see them again.

Measure your sales rankings against your actual book sales. You will soon be able to look at the rankings and gauge roughly how many books you have sold. It is exciting watching your book sell but don't waste too much time on it. Be careful not to get too fixated on the sales reports as it easy to spend hours every day looking to see if you have sold another book when you could be focusing on your writing or marketing. Remember that building sales and interest is a long-term venture. It will not happen overnight.

69 Set reachable and measurable goals

Marketing your book is a journey and as with most journeys, if you have no idea where you are going, you're unlikely to know when you are on the right road or when you've arrived. That's why goals are important. Set yourself a realistic goal but remember to be specific and keep your goals measurable. For example, becoming a bestseller within a year is not realistic and you will find it hard to measure on a daily or weekly basis.

+ For sales, use the reports that you receive from retailers or distributors and keep a spreadsheet of results.

+ For readership, you can send readers to a website or blog for additional information or interaction and use analytics provided by the site to measure traffic.

+ For interest, look at whether other people start to quote you and mention your ideas, and how often your blog or Twitter posts are forwarded by others.

+ For revenue goals, keep track of the profit from your e-book. You may have incurred expenses in getting your book to market, and by tracking this you'll know exactly when your book becomes profitable. Once you have cleared your production costs, you are earning a residual income while you sleep, but only if you put the effort in to market it while you're awake.

70   Print some sample books

Think seriously about printing a small number of your book using sites like Lulu.com or Createspace. They are simple and easy to use and you can carry a number of hard copies to your promotional appearances but be selective who you give them to. Your expenses will increase and your brand may suffer if you hand them out randomly. Remember you're looking for exposure for your e-book primarily but not everyone who you meet will be an avid e-book reader.

Use your hard copies to encourage reviews from within your media list. If you manage to get a piece in your local newspaper, then send the journalist a signed hard copy. You cannot have enough reviews of your books and if it costs you the price of a print-on-demand book, then it is worth every penny. Being a successful independent author means taking a long-term view. Many marketing efforts take months or years to come to fruition.

As you market your e-book, you will start to think of other ways to adapt the basics to your own circumstances. Keep thinking of how you can apply the successful promotions that you use to other groups or associations in different towns and cities.

71 *Develop your author website*

Your website should be fully functional, easy to navigate and consistently updated. To showcase your work is essential in a digital age. It is your online profile describing you and your book in your own words. If it is clear and professional then it is building your credibility as an author. Your website should be updated often, and it's a good idea to link your Facebook and Twitter pages so you can send one message to all your profiles at once. Your website can also be your shop window through which you can sell your books. If you'd prefer, you can link to your Amazon or Kobo pages so that you don't have to fulfil orders yourself. A well-designed website adds credence in your business and brand as an established author.

Reserve a domain name that includes your name and the title of your book. There are dozens of free hosting sites. Design your site to raise your profile and sell copies of your e-book; show your book covers and describe how your reviews are going. If you write fiction, be sure to describe your plot in compelling terms and add links to your readers' reviews. Use your website to promote your book by providing links to retail outlets. You may also choose to sell your book directly on your site and offer incentives such as free shipping, a limited-time offer or a special price for an autographed book. A website provides an opportunity to showcase your biographical details, positive reviews, endorsements and testimonials.

72   Inform your readers regularly about progress

As your sales grow and your book climbs the ranking, use your press contacts to inform their readers about your progression. Reasonably modest downloads can get your book into the genre charts and that is newsworthy. If the press are impressed and pick up your updates then it fosters viral marketing.

73   Keep press/media outlets updated

When planning your outreach, think about your target readers. What media do they watch, listen to, or read? You can reach a large number of people in a relatively short period of time through broadcast appearances on TV and radio shows, print and online media. Publicity is typically free and targeted to journalists, editors and producers at media outlets. Media personnel are always looking for a story, so you and your e-book could potentially provide them with a new storyline, background information, and other material.

A few years ago a former colleague of mine, Simon Gould, asked me to help him promote his debut novel, *Playing the Game*. We did and he followed the e-book techniques which launched my series and within a few months, his book was sitting at number four in the Kindle charts – not a genre-specific chart, but the overall charts. He sold 40,000 downloads in a few months. His success was newsworthy and he began riding the media interest and his book continued to sell. The BBC contacted him following an enquiry he made and asked about e-books and how he achieved his level of success. He mentioned my role and they sent a camera team and interviewed us both. The interviews were televised on the evening news programmes at six o'clock, nine o'clock and ten o'clock. Unfortunately for Simon, the piece didn't show the title of his book. It was more about the e-book phenomenon but they concentrated much of the item on my books. It was cruel because Simon had contacted them, but the following day *Soft Target* was back in the top twenty. The point is if you keep casting the net widely with interesting topics and timely updates, you will eventually catch fish... even if you have to share it with your mate!

74   *Make press releases professional and interesting*
Draft your own press release and make sure your regular updates to the media are professional and interesting. The basic press release is a brief description that presents the most newsworthy aspect of your book – the 'hook' – in an interesting way, for example, reaching number ten in the thriller sales charts.

An effective press release uses an attention-grabbing headline and lead paragraph. It is also free of advertising or commercialism. Subsequent paragraphs should include background information and other details that help put the newsworthiness of the story into perspective.

There should be a few paragraphs about the book, a brief paragraph about the author, and an action-filled excerpt from the book about a half page in length. Then, you should include your website address (or Amazon link) where the book can be ordered, and contact details for any press enquiries.

There are a number of free PR websites and online newswires where you can upload your press release, such as:

www.24-7pressrelease.com
www.clickpress.com
www.express-press-release.com
www.free-press-release-center.info.
www.free-press-releases.com
www.freepressreleases.co.uk
www.i-newswire.com
www.nosyjoe.com
www.pr.com
www.pressbox.co.uk
www.prlog.org
www.your-story.org

It usually takes two or three days before the press releases appear online as some PR websites may want to check them first before applauding them.

You should include copies of the latest press release in your press pack. Rather than issuing one press release only about the publication of your book, drip feed the media with periodic press releases that stimulate public interest and invite reviews and interviews. You can write book releases about upcoming speaking engagements, festival talks, future book signings, success in writing competitions, and any other newsworthy events related to your book.

75   Create a press kit
After becoming comfortable with basic publicity, you can begin more concerted and targeted efforts to reach media outside of your local

area. Create an informative press pack that has information about your book and why it is important to the outlet's audience. Include testimonials and a list of the topics you can discuss. When targeting the media, it's often beneficial to start locally and then broaden your scope.

Finally, look the part of a successful author by dressing smartly and professionally and using body language and posture effectively.

76   Organise radio interviews

Search your local radio's websites for the names and e-mail addresses of presenters and programme editors. If you contact them then add your author biography and one or two hooks into your book. If it is set locally and has places in it which their listeners can identify with, you could be invited for an interview. Be professional and polite in your approach and be patient waiting for a reply. They will contact you if they are interested.

If you do not feel comfortable talking to reporters or conducting radio and television interviews, then stick to print and online media. This type of exposure is equally important, particularly if you're camera shy. This includes newspapers, magazine, e-zines, newsletters and trade journals, most of which will have well-trafficked websites. Approach journalists in the same way you would approach producers, with a press kit written to the needs of their readers. Contact them to review your book, suggest a story or interview about you and your book, or offer to contribute some useful content to them. Be selective, starting with the media most likely to help your e-book reach your target audience. Follow up consistently and professionally.

77 Temper direct marketing

Direct marketing is a general form of communication that enables you to reach a targeted audience directly through one or more channels. Examples include e-mail, direct mail, catalogues and promotional letters. Postcards and bookmarks can also be effective since the message is seen immediately without opening an envelope or e-mail.

In all cases, direct marketing materials can be sent to a targeted list of potential buyers, and responses can be measured. With both e-mail and postal marketing campaigns, it is important to make sure your direct marketing material stands out and grabs the recipients' attention. With e-mail, the subject line is critical. Similarly, you can write a teaser on an envelope to entice the recipient to open the envelope. For postal mail, send a covering letter, sales piece, and some means for the recipient to respond such as a business reply card (BRC). Make an offer that will get the recipient to act quickly, such as directing them to your website to see a sample chapter or offering a free gift or autographed copy if they respond by a certain date.

78 Keep in regular contact with your readers

When you have a target market, you can reach it through personal communication. The major benefit of personal marketing is that you get immediate feedback about how well your message is getting through. It will also give you an opportunity to answer questions and close sales. When you're selling your books, you're also selling yourself as an author, so personal marketing is a great way to build your authentic author brand through direct and directive communication. Examples of personal marketing initiatives are bookstore signing events, launch parties, book tours, speaking events and personal presentations at libraries.

79 Practise and polish your presentations

Practise projecting your words and using your body language to evoke the sort of response that you'd like. While you'd use professional selling techniques when direct selling, be sure not to come over as too 'commercial' as that can put off potential readers.

80 Enter your e-book in literary competitions

If you are getting excellent reviews and positive feedback on your e-book then consider entering it in competitions. There are various award competitions for most kinds of books. Awards can focus on your book's cover design, content, marketing, sales and productivity, and even editing. There are awards for a range of genres including business, inspirational, crime fiction, fantasy, literary fiction, science-fiction, women's fiction and children's books. Winning, being shortlisted, long-listed or just nominated for an award is a newsworthy event and has many benefits, including increased exposure, greater kudos and credibility, and potential for testimonials and sales.

An element of personal satisfaction and validation comes with receiving awards as well. When you win an award, make the most of it! Mention the award in your literature, e-mail signature, business cards, postcards, website and letterhead. Describe your award in your press kits and include it in press releases or any display materials for in-person events.

81 Attend literary festivals and book fairs

There are many literary festivals, book fairs and trade shows to add to your diary. They are great events for networking and getting your face seen and your voice heard. They give you the chance to network with people in the industry, meet potential new readers, generate sales leads, close sales, research trends, build relationships, foster direct sales opportunities, generate publicity, or launch a new title.

82 Enlist help from your friends and family

Ask friends and family to distribute your postcards and bookmarks to their workmates. Warrington has many large call centres with thousands of employees and I used my contacts there to great effect, handing out and electronically distributing promotional material through various companies' internal e-mail systems. Don't wait for your friends to offer to help. Rather, take the initiative and ask if they can recommend your book to others.

5

Other Resources
for e-book Marketing

83   Join Goodreads.com

Build up your profile on Goodreads as a reviewer as well as an author.
You can add all the classics that you have read and write a quick
review of them. Add other authors as friends and invite them to swap
reviews of your book. Make sure that you are positive. It is better not
to leave a review than to leave a poor one.

84   Join Kindleboards.com

Kindleboards is the biggest Kindle forum on the internet and there are
hundreds of forums and groups to interact with. The same rules apply
here as mentioned before – don't ram your book down people's
throats. Develop your contacts and be constructive and gregarious.

85   Adapt your e-book to other markets and formats

I turned six of my thrillers into young adult novels by taking out any
abusive language and toning down the violence. If you can do that then
it is a quick and simple exercise, as teenagers love exciting books and
they tend to be very active on social networks and have a large peer
group to spread the word about your books.

86   Set up outposts

Outposts depend on your book's subject matter and they will be placed where people interested in your subject have a tendency to congregate. You can find effective outposts in the following places.

+ Facebook fan pages.

+ Photosharing sites, including photostream on Flickr.com, especially if you have many local places of interest in your novel.

+ Bookmarking sites like StumbleUpon.com

+ Specialised niche sites like those on Ning.com

You can monitor their effectiveness.

87 Consider using Apex Reviews

I used Apex Reviews to gain a review and develop a video trailer for one of my books. They charged about £30 for a professional review and a good video. They often run special offers and are well worth a look. With a video, brevity is the key. Keep it short, simple, professional, entertaining and informative.

88 Tag your e-book to similar books

Identify books that are similar to yours and tag your book to it. You will see the tag lines halfway down the Amazon page. Tagging is a great way to bring your book up when readers search a specific genre. Tags can help you find items on Amazon and provide an easy way for you to 'remember' and classify items for later recall.

89 Add your author biography to all your profiles

As an author, you are selling yourself as a product, so it is important to start making the right brand impressions early. Think about who you know and about your background in terms of how it can help you sell more books.

90   Use the 'Tell Your Fans' feature to full effect

With the tools built into the fan page, Facebook allows you to import your contacts from Hotmail, Yahoo!, etc. This is useful when you're just starting out and want to tell people you already know about your e-book and your growing fan base.

91   Set up a Facebook fan page

Once you have established a fan base, set up a Facebook fan page. This is not essential until you are approaching 5,000 friends but it is worth planning well before you reach that level. Promoting your fan page is a campaign in itself so plan a few days to work on it. Put your fan page URL in your e-mail signature. How many e-mails do you send each day? Now imagine each e-mail you send is a chance for someone new to find out about your amazing fan page! Write a blog post about your new fan page.

Give your readers five compelling reasons why they should join your fan page. Don't beg; just give the reasons why they'll benefit. New fans are going to join and frequent your fan page if they feel they have something to gain by doing so.

92   Tag well-trafficked fan pages

By tagging to popular fan pages their fans may see your page and you may get some cross-traffic and cross-promotion.

93   Ask Twitter followers to join your fan page

Twitter followers can find you on Facebook. Give some convincing reasons why your Tweeters should also join your Facebook community. If Twitter is the new water cooler, think of your fan page as an invitation to come in and chat. For example, tweet something like, 'Wanting more conversation than 140 characters will allow? Join us on Facebook at http://fb.me/fanpage.' A simple request will get results.

94   Put a fan page widget on your blog or website

You'll be amazed at how many people simply don't know about your fan page. Putting a widget on your website (i.e. your home base) will get it in front of all of your website visitors.

95   Customise your fan page URL

Vanity URLs are a fantastic way to make your fan page memorable. 'Check out this awesome fan page http://facebook.com/awesomefan page.'

96   Put your fan page URL on all your literature

Add your URL to your business cards, bookmarks and the back cover of your e-book. Combine offline and online promotion by letting the people you meet in real life know about your fan page.

97   Link to your fan page on your Facebook profile

Add a link under the 'links' section. This is a 'soft sell' of sorts, letting your friends passively know about your page.

98   Ask fans to post a link on their profile

As long as you don't ask them to post links too often, people tend to be glad to help. Leverage the power of your existing audience and see the results.

99   Add to your Twitter profile background

Lots of tweeters still use the Twitter web-based version and your profile background is a prime piece of web real estate. Cross-media market using one social network to promote another.

100   Add your e-book to IPR Licensing

If your e-book is self-published, it may be worth joining international websites which can sell the foreign rights to your book such as IPR Licensing (*www.iprlicensing.co.uk*) as well as those listed in Appendix 5 of this book.

6

The Growth and Future
of e-books

The rapid growth of e-books has largely been driven by problems within the print book industry. Firstly, as authors know all too well, many traditional publishers will not accept non-agented or unsolicited submissions and because agents are oversubscribed and tend to work on a commission-only basis, they generally offer to represent authors with the biggest name each time.

Secondly, book retailers are struggling and printed books are increasingly costly and take a while to arrive, whereas e-books can be bought for less and downloaded straight away.

Thirdly, the increase of e-books has driven the growth and reduction in cost of e-readers, which can hold multiple e-books for you to read, thereby giving you more choice while travelling or on holiday.

Fourthly, e-books don't require stocking or the prospect of sales returns, so publishers are increasingly publishing new books in digital format to test the market and then printing the most successful ones.

Moreover, e-books can be produced and published more quickly than print books, and thus can be turned out to meet current demand. For example, when the banking crisis occurred in the UK, Mark Leigh wrote and published his humorous *Crash! The Official Bankers Joke Book* within a week.

So, if e-books provide authors with a direct route to market, are much less costly, can be downloaded immediately, can be easily stored in e-readers and read at any time, don't require stocking or the risk of returns, can be produced and published within days, and bring a handy residual income, it seems likely that they will continue to increase year on year and take a larger share of the book market.

However, print book aficionados will say there's nothing like holding a paperback in your hands and it is difficult reading books off the internet or on handheld electronic and mobile devices.

What I would say is the industry is trying to play catch-up to adapt to the growth in e-books, to incorporate them into their business models. I don't think traditional publishers will go out of business or that printed books will become obsolete, but I do think the growth of the e-book industry will put pressure on retailers to lower their margins and place demands on publishers to capture more of this market which is quickly passing them by.

Will e-books gradually overtake tree-books? I think e-books will take over the lion's share of the market and sooner than many may think, as e-readers improve and become more accessible. Still, the key question is: will the emergence of e-books improve the industry and make it less insular and bring quality back to the fore? I do think that it will.

Appendix 1

Checklist of 100 Top-Selling Tips

1 Write hooks into your e-book

2 Mention real places in your book

3 Use real names to build reader loyalty

4 Keep your vocabulary simple and concise

5 Write an exciting first line, paragraph and chapter

6 Keep the story flowing – don't be over-descriptive

7 Use an e-book template, and add a 'Look Inside'

8 Reflect the genre and content in the book title

9 Judge your book by its cover

10 Write a catchy back cover synopsis

11 Create an interesting preview

12 Build a relationship with your readers

13 Choose your digital platform carefully

14 Sell through multiple e-bookstores/directories

15 Create a sales page optimised for search engines

16 Make the book available in multiple file formats

17 Use E-Junkie for e-book delivery and affiliates

18 Price your book intelligently

19 Avoid under-pricing your book

20 Set low price point for your first book

21 Experiment with pricing and monitor closely

22 Charge what you would pay for the book

23   Base pricing on quality, not on book length

24   Keep a checklist of promotional activity

25   Do not spend any money on advertising

26   Seek out third-party endorsements

27   Build your profession into your Facebook name

28   Build your profile positively

29   Join relevant online groups

30   Update and inform readers about your books

31   Increase your friends/contacts and set up an event

32   Keep your author page fun and interesting

33   Add 'author' or 'writer' to your Twitter username

34   Use Twitterific

35   Search out relevant contacts in book world

36   Search the list pages

37   Keep an eye on followers

38   Tweet useful links and ideas

39   Pick up followers with useful content

40   Retweet other authors

41   Build trust with your tweets

42   Use postings links and photographs

43   Join LinkedIn

44   Join marketing groups and book forums

45   Link your LinkedIn account to other accounts

46   Join MySpace, Ning, Bebo and video-sharing sites

47   Put your protagonist on Facebook and Twitter

48   Join social networks

49   Join social bookmarking sites

50   Connect with vendors and marketers

51   Avoid pay-per-click

52   Write a blog and keep it current

53   Promote your book professionally

54   Seek reviews and reply to all of them

55   Offer limited period discounts and create bundles

56   Build a loyal readership

57   Offer the first chapter for free

58   Search local directories for relevant links

59   Contact local press

60   Write personalised letters to local venues

61   Tailor presentations to book writing

62   Seek out regional associations

63   Contact writing groups

64   Contact local and regional libraries

65   Leave a gift

66   Ensure promotional materials are current

67   Leave your Facebook and Twitter details

68   Monitor sales closely

69   Set reachable and measurable goals

70   Print some sample books

71   Develop your author website

72   Inform your readers regularly about progress

73   Keep press/media outlets updated

74   Make press releases professional and interesting

75   Create a press kit

76   Organise radio interviews

77   Temper direct marketing

78   Keep in regular contact with your readers

79   Practise and polish your presentations

80   Enter your e-book in literary competitions

81   Attend literary festivals and book fairs

82   Enlist help from your friends and family

83   Join Goodreads.com

84   Join Kindleboards.com

85   Adapt your e-book to other markets and formats

86   Set up outposts

Appendix 2
UK Style Guide

ABBREVIATIONS AND CONTRACTIONS

Use the full point after abbreviations and contractions only where the last letter is not the final letter of the word: No., Capt., a.m., p.m., i.e., e.g. (upper- and lower-case). And for personal initials: W. B. Yeats.

The full point is omitted thus: Mr, Dr, St, Ltd; after sets of initials: BBC, NATO, MP and also after abbreviated units of measurement: ft, in, m, km, lb, g.

CAPITALISATION

Aim for the minimum use of capitalisation. Generally, however, the following are capitalised.

Specific organisations and groups, institutions and religious bodies: the Labour Party, but the party, the Church believes, but the church nearby, Buddhism, Buddhist, Islam, Muslim.

Titles and ranks where a specific individual is named: Queen Charlotte, but a queen, all lords, no bishops, kings of England.

Historical periods, wars and economic or political periods: Neolithic, Stone Age, the Second World War, the Depression.

Geographical locations recognised as social/political regions: the Midlands, the West Country, but the north, the south-west.

FIGURES AND NUMBERS

Write numbers below 100 in words (except where the author is comparing numbers or recording a unit of measurement); 100 and above as numerals: 2 cats and 144 dogs, six dogs and eighty-six cats; I could see for 6 miles.

For collective numbers use the least number of figures possible: 1944–5, 1986–93, 1997–2003. But note: 1990–95, 16–17, 116–17.

Set dates: 1 February 1950, in the late nineteenth century (but late-nineteenth century war), the eighties, the 1980s, but in the 1970s and '80s. AD (preceding date) and BC (following date).

Set times of the day: four o'clock, 11.15 a.m., 7.45 p.m., a quarter to eight, half past nine.

ITALICS

Use italics for the titles of books, book-length poems, newspapers and magazines; works of performed art, television and radio programmes; names of ships.

Follow *The Oxford Guide to Style* for foreign and anglicised words and use italics for emphasis sparingly.

LAYOUT

The first line of a chapter should normally be set full out. A new section, following a one-line space, also should be set full out. Text which follows an extract or verse quote, also full out, unless this impairs the sense, in which case it should be indented as a new paragraph.

However, the layout of headings, quotations and lists, the order and content of preliminary matter, and the construction of notes and references must be retained.

PUNCTUATION

Aim to 'correct grammar, to impose consistency, and to clarify – not alter – meaning'. All general rules are dealt with in *The Oxford Guide to Style*. Some points that may cause difficulty are as follows.

Apostrophe

Possessives: The inclusion or omission of the possessive s should be decided on the grounds of euphony; this means that some possessives will have an s and some will not, but there should be some system. *The Oxford Guide Style* recommends that (except in ancient names) 's should be used in all monosyllables and disyllables, and in longer words accented on the penultimate syllable. Also, 's should be used except when the last syllable of the word is pronounced iz: Bridges', Moses', but James's, Thomas's.

Watch out for the incorrect apostrophe in its, yours, ours, theirs, hers.

Plurals: Do not use the apostrophe when creating plurals: the Joneses (not the Jones's); the 1990s (not the 1990's); QCs (not QC's). Do not employ what is sometimes known as the 'greengrocer's apostrophe': orange's for oranges and cauli's for cauliflowers.

No apostrophe in phone, plane, bus, flu etc.

Dashes and ellipses

For parenthetical dashes, use spaced en rules.

For the omission of part of a word, or for abruptly curtailed speech, use a closed-up em rule.

For the omission of a whole word, use a spaced em rule.

Ellipses should be spaced thus… with a full point at the end of the sentence, if relevant.

Hyphenation

Do not hyphenate unnecessarily.

Use hyphens to avoid ambiguity: a little used car or a little-used car; when employing words attributively: an ill-informed person; in phrasal compounds: jack-in-the-box; in compound adjectives preceding a noun: working-class hero; where part of the compound is a measurement: 9-mile run.

Omit hyphens when employing words predicatively: that person is ill informed; when the first word of the compound is an adverb: widely known facts; or where the compound is a name: Iron Age fort.

Quotations

Preferably use single quotation marks, reserving double quotes for a quote within a quote but the decision is the author's.

Place punctuation marks in relation to quotation marks according to sense. The closing inverted comma precedes all punctuation except an exclamation mark, question mark, dash or ellipsis belonging to the quotation. Where a full sentence, with an initial capital, is quoted at the end of a main (author's) sentence, the full point should precede the inverted comma.

In dialogue the punctuation is always placed inside the punctuation marks: 'It is,' he said, 'a great album.'

Closing parenthesis

A full point should precede a closing parenthesis only if the parentheses enclose a complete sentence which is not part of a longer sentence. A question mark or exclamation mark may precede or follow a closing parenthesis as the sense demands. A comma, colon, semicolon or a parenthetical dash should never precede a closing parenthesis.

SPELLING

Use the *Shorter Oxford English Dictionary*. There is an online dictionary resource from OUP: *www.askoxford.com* or refer to The *Oxford Guide to Style* for alternative spellings, unusual words or short foreign phrases. Collective nouns are singular, e.g. company, government. Verbs used with them must also be singular.

Optional endings: -ise or -ize (author's choice).

Retain American spelling for proper names: Pearl Harbor, Rockefeller Center.

Appendix 3
UK Writers' Groups and Workshops

Writers' group	E-mail
Alistair Paterson	prism.atic@virgin.net
Alston Hall College	alstonhall.general2@lancashire.gov.uk
Andover Writers' Workshop	admin@andoverwriters.co.uk
Anglia Ruskin University	answers@anglia.ac.uk
Angus Writers' Circle	nicolasjw@hotmail.co.uk
Ann Newbegin	annnewbegin@hotmail.com
Apples and Snakes	george@applesandsnakes.org
Apples and Snakes	irenosen@applesandsnakes.org
Apples and Snakes East Midlands	stephanie@applesandsnakes.org
Apples and Snakes West Midlands	natasha@applesandsnakes.org
Armagh Writers' Group	Kevin@abcwritersnetwork.co.uk
Ashford Writers	yym@btopenworld.com
Ashton-in-Makerfield Writers' and Literary Club Wood	woodwigan@aol.com
Ayr Writers' Club	f.mcfadzean@btinternet.com
Bangor Cellar Group	lowri_ann@hotmail.com
Bath Spa Univ. College	enquiries@bathspa.ac.uk
Bath Writers' Group	clancy.inc@blueyonder.co.uk
Battersea Writers' Group	jasonyoung72@yahoo.com
Belstead House	belstead.house@educ.suffolkcc.gov.uk
Birmingham Group	join.Bwg@googlemail.com
Bournemouth University	enquiries@bournemouth.ac.uk

Bradford Writers' Circle	bradfordwriterscircle@hotmail.com
Brentwood Writers' Circle	ena.love@tiscali.co.uk
Bridgend Writers' Circle	boswell258@talktalk.net
Brighter Writers	Brighter_writers@btinternet.com
Brumqueerink	BrumQueerInk@aol.com
Burton Manor	george.cooke@burtonmanor.com
Cambridge Wordfest	admin@cambridgewordfest.co.uk
Cambridge Writers	cambridgewriters@hotmail.com
Cannon Poets	info@cannonpoets.co.uk
Cardiff Centre for Lifelong Learning	train@cardiff.ac.uk
Cardiff Writers' Circle	niva@nivapete.freeserve.co.uk
Cecily Bomberg	cecily@bombergwriting.co.uk
Chandlers Ford Writers	info@wyvernwriters.co.uk
Charnwood Arts	kevr@charnwoodarts.com
Chelmsford Writers	secretary@chelmsfordwriters.org.uk
Cheltenham Writers' Circle	carol.sandiford@blueyonder.co.uk
Chiltern Writers	info@chilternwriters.org
Chris Leonard	mail@chris-leonard-writing.co.uk
Chrysalis to Butterfly – The Poet in You	jay@ramsay3892.fsnet.co.uk
City Lit	infoline@citylit.ac.uk
City University	enquiries@city.ac.uk
Company of Writers	mazzy@unfurling.net
Coventry Writers' Group	krismonsen@btinternet.com
Creative Ink	creative.ink@lycos.co.uk
Creative Writers' Network	info@creativewritersnetwork.org
Creative Writes	creativewrites@hotmail.co.uk
Creative Writing Ink	enquiries@oca-uk.com
Crescent Arts Centre Writers' Workshops	info@crescentarts.org
Croydon Writers' Circle	battenberg@yahoo.co.uk

Dean Writers' Circle	rachel.hayward@tesco.net
Della Galton	info@dellagalton.co.uk
Denman College	hq@nfwi.org.uk
Derwent Writers	Mail@DerwentWriters.co.uk
DESIblitz Writing Group	editor@desiblitz.com
Dillington House	dillington@somerset.gov.uk
Dunholme Writers	john@bloodaxe.co.uk
East Anglian Writers	chair@eastanglianwriters.org.uk
East Dulwich Group	info@edwg.co.uk
Edinburgh University	cce@ed.ac.uk
Edinburgh Writers' Club	kate.blackadder@talk21.com
Elaine Everest	elaineeverest@aol.com
Ellipsis Writing Group	feedback@ellipsisWriting.org.uk
Euphoric ink	info@euphoricink.co.uk
Euroscript	ask@euroscript.co.uk
Eve Menezes Cunningham	eve@applecoaching.com
Exiled Writers	Jennifer@exiledwriters.fsnet.co.uk
Falmouth Poetry Group	pdshuttle@aol.com
Fareham Writers	enquiries@farehamwriters.co.uk
Farncombe Estate Centre	enquiries@FarncombeEstate.co.uk
Felixstowe Scribblers	scribblers@ntlworld.com
Fiction City	fictioncity@gmail.com
Fiction Writing Workshop	louise_gethin@hotmail.com
Fire in the Head Creative Writing Programme	roselle@fire-in-the-head.co.uk
Free Spirit Writers	freespiritwriters@tesco.net
Gamlingay and District Writers' Group	tracey@twotodes.seriouslyinternet.com
Gloswordshop	gloswordshop@blueyonder.co.uk
Grace Dieu Writers' Circle	tonygutteridge@live.com
Guildford Writers	margravejen@googlemail.com
Hackney and East London Creative	

Writing Circle	nerosiri@yahoo.co.uk
Harlow Writers Workshop	anne.neuhaus@ntlworld.com
Harrow Writers' Circle	ocmonteiro@hotmail.com
Hastings Writers' Group	hastingswritersgroup@gmail.com
Higham Hall College	admin@highamhall.com
Highgreen Arts	highgreenarts@aol.com
Hills Road Sixth Form	jaberdour@hillsroad.ac.uk
Hogs Back Writers	secretary@hbw.org.uk
Institute of Continuing Ed.	aeb53@cam.ac.uk
Interchange @ IDL (Bradford Network)	joedot@blueyonder.co.uk
Katherine Gallagher	mail@katherine-gallagher.com
King Alfred's College	press@winchester.ac.uk
King's Lynn Writers' Circle	enquiries@lynnwriters.org.uk
Knuston Hall College for Adult Education	enquiries@knustonhall.org.uk
Lancaster University	v.tyrrell@lancaster.ac.uk
Learn Writing	info@learnwriting.co.uk
Leeds Writers' Circle	chair@leedswriterscircle.co.uk
Leicester Poetry Society	david.bircumshaw@ntlworld.com
Leicester Writers' Club	rod@rodduncan.co.uk
Lincoln Phoenix Circle	allens.athome@virgin.net
Linda James	writingunderwater@tiscali.co.uk
London Comedy Writers	londoncomedywriters@gmail.com
London Writers' Café	lisagoll@hotmail.com
London Writers' Workshops	londonwritersworkshop @hotmail.co.uk
London Writing Workshops	londonwritingworkshops @googlemail.com
Magnetic North	pgfreeman@yahoo.com
Malvern Writers' Circle	malvernwriterscircle@hotmail.co.uk
Marylebone Group	jkispal@hotmail.com

Maureen Osborne	Maureen@nightowl.wanadoo.co.uk
Mead Kerr Limited	info@meadkerr.com
Missenden Abbey Adult Learning Centre	eva.nj@missendenabbey.ltd.uk
Mole Valley Poets	membershipsecretary@molevalleypoets.co.uk
Mole Valley Scriptwriting	tim@molevalleyscripts.co.uk
Monday Night Group	info@mondaynightgroup.org.uk
N16 Writers and Readers	sue.gee@tiscali.co.uk
National TV School	info@nfts.co.uk
Neath Writers' Group	llewelyn37@talktalk.net
New Rivers Group	duffusjj@hotmail.com
Newham Workshop	nwwstjohns@googlemail.com
Norden Farm Creative Writers	matthew.biss@nordenfarm.org
North Herts Writers Circle	Victoria@snelling00.vispa.com
North London Group	northlondonwriters@yahoo.co.uk
Northampton Group	piedpiperrecords@aol.com
Northampton Lit. Group	dizsampson@supanet.com
Northwest Playwrights	newplaysnw@hotmail.com
Nottingham Trent Univ.	its.servicedesk@ntu.ac.uk
Nuffield Theatre Group	info@nuffieldtheatre.co.uk
Oxford Film and Video Makers	geron@ofvm.org
Petersfield Workshop	susanneleigh@gmail.com
Pier Playwrights	admin@newwritingsouth.com
Pitshanger Poets	nala.ques@virgin.net
Plymouth Library Group	plymouthproprietarywriters@googlemail.com
PMA Training	training@pma-group.com
Poetry at The Troubadour	info@troubadour.co.uk
Poole Writers' Circle	enquires@writerspoole.co.uk
Queen's Park Writers	QueensParkWriters@gmail.com
Queen's University	e.larrissy@qub.ac.uk

Redwell Writers	info@redwellwriters.org
Richmond Adult Community College	info@racc.ac.uk
Richmond Writers' Circle	info@richmondwriterscircle.org.uk
Ripon Writers' Group	maggie@maggiecobbett.co.uk
Roehampton University	enquiries@roehampton.ac.uk
Royal Holloway	drama@rhul.ac.uk
Ruskin College	enquiries@ruskin.ac.uk
Scarborough Society	Katie@savonarola.fsnet.co.uk
Script Yorkshire	admin@scriptyorkshire.co.uk
Scriveners	scriveners@lycos.co.uk
Sheffield Hallam University	enquiries@shu.ac.uk
Shepherds Bush Group	anjan@anjansaha.com
South West Writers	southwestwriters@yahoo.com
South Yardley Creative Writing Group	spcnac@yahoo.co.uk
Southend Poetry Group	dorothy@southendpoetry.co.uk
Southport Writers' Circle	southportwriterscircle@yahoo.co.uk
Spread the Word	info@spreadtheword.org.uk
Spring Tides Group	listmanager@northeastwriters.co.uk
St Helens Writers' Circle	gavin@citadel.org.uk
Stanton Guildhouse	info@stantonguildhouse.org.uk
Strathkelvin Writers	enquiries@strathkelvinwriters.org
Suffolk Poetry Society	ian@poetryanglia.org
Sutton Writers' Circle	teresa.tipping@hotmail.com
Swan Playwrights	webmaster@swanplaywrights.co.uk
Teifi Scribblers	simone@simonemb.com
Tenbury Writers' Group	sallytenbury@yahoo.com
Thames ValleyCircle	sawdonsmith@hotmail.com
Thameside Poetry Workshop	fionamoore@aetos.freeserve.co.uk
Thatcham Writers	martha@thatchamwriters.co.uk
The Arvon Foundation	hurst@arvonfoundation.org

The Arvon Foundation	m-mhor@arvonfoundation.org
The Arvon Foundation	t-barton@arvonfoundation.org
The Complete Creative Writing Course	maggie@writingcourses.org.uk
The Fielding Programme	info@fieldingprogramme.com
The Goldfish Bowl	admin@writingincircles.co.uk
The Indian King Poets	indianking@btconnect.com
The Inklings	aninkling@blueyonder.co.uk
The Inn Scribers	lesleymjames@talktalk.net
The Medway Mermaids	rockyhorror75@hotmail.com
The Norwegian Writing Circle in London	brit.warren@btinternet.com
The Plough Group	sarah.lawson1@btinternet.com
The Poetry Business	poetrybusiness@gmail.com
The Windows Project	windowsproject@btinternet.com
The Write Coach	bekki@thewritecoach.co.uk
Ty Newydd	post@tynewydd.org
University of Newcastle upon Tyne	press.office@ncl.ac.uk
University College Chichester	website@chi.ac.uk
University College Falmouth	shortcourses@falmouth.ac.uk
University of Aberystwyth	mss@aber.ac.uk
University of Bradford	press@bradford.ac.uk
University of Bristol	Tom.Sperlinger@bristol.ac.uk
University of Cumbria	admissionslancaster@cumbria.ac.uk
University of Derby	askadmissions@derby.ac.uk
University of East Anglia	admissions@uea.ac.uk
University of Exeter	s.d.franklin@exeter.ac.uk
University of Glamorgan	press@glam.ac.uk
University of Glasgow	dace-query@educ.gla.ac.uk
University of Hull	m.p.arnold@hull.ac.uk
University of Kent at Canterbury	cfl@kent.ac.uk
University of Leeds	business@leeds.ac.uk

University of Liverpool	kate.spark@liv.ac.uk
University of Liverpool Creative Writing Society	Thomas.mcbride2@sky.com
University of Oxford	john.ballam@conted.ox.ac.uk
University of Plymouth	prospectus@plymouth.ac.uk
University of Salford	U.K.Hurley@salford.ac.uk
University of St Andrews	english@st-andrews.ac.uk
University of the Arts	info@arts.ac.uk
University of Warwick	engd@warwick.ac.uk
University of Westminster	course-enquiries@westminster.ac.uk
Verulam Writers' Circle	info@verulamwriterscircle.org.uk
W.E.A.	info.alingtonhouse@gmail.com
Walsall Writers' Circle	walsall.writerscircle@hotmail.co.uk
Walton Wordsmiths	words@stickler.org.uk
Ware Poets	rockpress@ntlworld.com
Watford Writers	watfordwriters@gmail.com
Ways with Words	admin@wayswithwords.co.uk
Westminster Writers	westminsterwriters@hotmail.com
Wight Fair Writers' Circle	carolbridgestock@hotmail.com
Willesden Green Group	willesdengreenlibrary@brent.gov.uk
Women's Ink Writing	womensink@hotmail.com
Woodham Scribblers	webmaster@woodhamscribblers.co.uk
Worcester Writers' Circle	secretary@worcesterwriters.org.uk
Word for Word	wordforword@london.com
Wordplay	tonya@wordplay.org.uk
WordWatchers	peterpheasant@aol.com
Write Now	george@wickerswork.co.uk
Write of Eden	lynette54uk@yahoo.co.uk
Writeopia	writeopia@gmail.com
Writergrrls	londonwritergrrls-subscribe@ yahoogroups.com
Writers Holiday Caerleon	Enquiries@writersholiday.net

Writers Of Our Age	pjbruce@ukonline.co.uk
Writers Together	writers.together@ntlworld.com
Writers' and Poets' Circle	veronicaspaintbox@yahoo.co.uk
Writers' Centre Norwich	info@writerscentrenorwich.org.uk
Writers' Workshops	Barbara.Large@winchester.ac.uk
Writing in Wales	rebeccajwoods@blueyonder.co.uk
Writtenwords.net	henrietta@writtenwords.net

Online forums

Abbeydale Writers
Aberdeen Writers' Circle
Commonword
Initialize Films
Liberato Breakaway Writing Courses
Marsh Ink Writers' Group
Petersfield Writers Circle
Rising Brook Writers
Riverside Writers
ScriptTank
Shaun Levin
South Manchester Writers' Workshop
Southwest Scriptwriters
Survivors Poetry
Sussex Playwrights Club
The Institute
The Poetry School
The Poetry Society's Poetry Café
The T Party
The Writers Summer School at Swanwick
Training and Performance Showcase (TAPS)
Writing Events Bath
Write in Bexley

Appendix 4
UK Libraries

English counties

Buckinghamshire	lib-ahq@buckscc.gov.uk
Cambridgeshire	your.library@cambridgeshire.gov.uk
Cheshire	libraries@cheshiresharedservices.gov.uk
Devon	phil.bater@devon.gov.uk and/or
	jean.hall@devon.gov.uk
East Sussex	chris.desmond@eastsussex.gov.uk
Essex	answers.direct@essex.gov.uk
Gateshead	heleneddon@gateshead.gov.uk
Hampshire	heritage@hants.gov.uk
Hertfordshire	hertsdirect@herts.gov.uk
Leicestershire	countyhalllibrary@leics.gov.uk
Manchester	j.shadbolt@manchester.gov.uk
Newcastle	information@newcastle.gov.uk
Norfolk	info.services.dcs@norfolk.gov.uk
North Yorkshire	roland.walls@northyorks.gov.uk
Northamptonshire	centlib@northamptonshire.gov.uk
Nottinghamshire	contactlibraries@nottscc.gov.uk
Portsmouth	libraries@portsmouthcc.gov.uk
Shropshire	rob.woodward@shropshire.gov.uk
South Yorkshire	centrallending.library@sheffield.gov.uk
Suffolk	libraries.direct@suffolk.gov.uk
Surrey	libraries@surrey.gov.uk

Warwickshire	katemackie@warwickshire.gov.uk
West Sussex	libraries@westsussex.gov.uk
Wiltshire	jessica.phillips@wiltshire.gov.uk
Worcestershire	david.pearson@worcestershire.gov.uk

Wales

Anglesey	rfrxlh@anglesey.gov.uk
Cardiff	centrallibrary@cardiff.gov.uk
Carmarthenshire	shmorgan@carmarthenshire.gov.uk
Ceredigion	gareth.griffiths@ceredigion.gov.uk
Conwy	Cheryl.hesketh@conwy.gov.uk
	Chris.Jones@conwy.gov.uk
Gwynedd	covered by Conwy and Anglesey
Monmouthshire	juliagreenway@monmouthshire.gov.uk
Newport	Rhodri.matthews@newport.gov.uk
Pembrokeshire	gill.gilliland@pembrokeshire.gov.uk
Powys	louise.ingham@powys.gov.uk
Swansea	Julie.clement@swansea.gov.uk

Scotland

Bute and Argyll	sue.fortune@argyll-bute.gov.uk
Clackmannanshire	libraries@clacks.gov.uk
Dumfries and Galloway	anne.rinaldi@dumgal.gov.uk
Dundee	Janis.milne@leisureandculturedundee.com
East Ayrshire	libraries@east-ayrshire.gov.uk
East Dunbartonshire	eryl.morris@eastdunbarton.gov.uk
East Lothian	ahunter@eastlothian.gov.uk
Edinburgh	jenny.hayes@edinburgh.gov.uk
Fife	Christine.cook@fife.gov.uk
Glasgow	gerry.torley@glasgowlife.org.uk
Highlands	Alison.forrest@highlifehighland.com

Inverclyde	john.rushton@inverclyde.gov.uk
Inverness	june.mcmillan@highlifehighland.com
Midlothian	library.hq@midlothian.gov.uk
North Ayrshire	AMcallister@north-ayrshire.gov.uk
North Lanarkshire	walesc@northlan.gov.uk
Perth and Kinross	ammacdonald@pkc.gov.uk
S. Lanarkshire	heather.maclean@library.slanark.org.uk
Scottish Borders	knairn@scotborders.gov.uk
Shetland Isles	Karen.fraser@shetland.gov.uk
Stirling	mcarav@stirling.gov.uk
West	Mary.MacLean@west-dunbarton.gov.uk

London boroughs

Barking and Dagenham	zoinul.abidin@lbbd.gov.uk
Barnet	mandy.stebbings@barnet.gov.uk
Brent	emma.palmer@brent.gov.uk
Bromley	janet.pullan@bromley.gov.uk
Ealing	jwilliams@ealing.gov.uk
Greenwich	jean.wright@greenwich.gov.uk
Hackney	monica.sever@hackney.gov.uk
Harrow	simon.smith@harrow.gov.uk
Havering	matthew.wright@havering.gov.uk
Hillingdon	wrussell@hillingdon.gov.uk
Hounslow	elaine.collier@laing.com
Kingston	alison.townsend@rbk.kingston.gov.uk
Lewisham	mark.challen@lewisham.gov.uk or alan.morrison@lewisham.gov.uk
Newham	richard.durack@newham.gov.uk
Redbridge	nick.dobson@visionrcl.org.uk
Richmond	rosie.piasecki@richmond.gov.uk
Southwark	soulaf.rizki@southwark.gov.uk

Sutton	karyn.isaac@sutton.gov.uk
Tower Hamlets	kate.pitman@towerhamlets.gov.uk
Wandsworth	gread@wandsworth.gov.uk

Miscellaneous

Denbighshire	jeff.harrison@denbighshire.gov.uk
Guernsey	sue.laker@priaulxlibrary.co.uk
Jersey	je.library@gov.je
Kingston upon Hull	Jessica.heathley@hullcc.gov.uk
Stockton on Tees	penny.slee@stockton.gov.uk

Appendix 5
Foreign Rights Websites

http://www.cup.columbia.edu/press/sub.html
http://everyonewhosanyone.com/aguk2.html
http://www.escritores.org/recursos/agentes.htm
http://www.esslinger-verlag.de/foreign/agencies.php
http://www.loewe-verlag.de/rights/agencies.html
http://www.mcclelland.com/rights/agents.html
http://www.obrien.ie/contact.cfm?list=lite
http://www.randomhouse.ca/rights/foreign.html
http://www.temple.edu/tempress/foreign_rights.html
http://www.swayzeagency.com/aboutus.html

Glossary of Terms

Affiliate Marketing: Performance-based marketing in which other sites are rewarded for each visitor or customer brought about by its own marketing effort.

Amazon.com: The leading online retailer of books in the world today.

Author Brand: How much your books are recognised and how well you are known as a published author.

Author Platform: How well-positioned you are to sell and market your book, including your readership/fan base, availability/visibility and authority to help your book reach its intended target audience.

Bebo.com: An acronym for 'Blog Early, Blog Often'. Bebo is a social networking site that has a section dedicated to writers called *Bebo Authors*.

Blog (short for *web log*): Online journal updated regularly and reflecting the author's interests and current activities.

BranchOut: Facebook.com application designed for networking professionally.

Calibre-e-book.com: A free and open source e-book library management application.

Clickbank: The internet's leading retailer of digital products including e-books.

Digital download: The process of copying an e-book to a computer or e-reader (i.e. handheld devices like Nook and Kindle).

Direct marketing: Sending and selling your book directly to readers and retailers, typically through e-mail, telephone, post or fax.

e-book: A book-length publication in digital format, consisting of text, images, or both, and produced on, published through, and readable on computers or other electronic devices.

E-commerce: Online selling, typically involving the acceptance of credit card details, site security for online transactions, and an order fulfilment process in place.

E-Junkie.com: A copy and paste, hosted shopping cart and digital delivery service which includes e-books.

e-reader (electronic reader): Hand-held device such as Kindle, iPad, Nook, iPhone, Sony Reader and Kobo to download and read e-books.

e-tailer: Online retailer like Amazon and Barnes & Noble for listing and selling e-books.

Facebook.com: Social networking website on which you can add friends to your Facebook page and send them messages, alerting them about new events in your life, such as the publication of your e-book.

Fan page: A facility on Facebook that enables you to build up a following for your e-book by sending regular updates to an unlimited number of people, and keep the focus on the organisation without revealing the administrator (unless you want to).

Flickr.com: An image hosting and video hosting website, web services suite, and online community.

Gather.com: A social networking website designed to encourage interaction through various social, political and cultural topics.

Goodreads.com: A privately-run social cataloguing website which permits individuals to sign up and register books to create their library catalogues and reading lists. It also allows users to create their own groups of book suggestions and discussion topics.

Google adwords: Pay-per-click advertising and site-targeted advertising for text, banner, and rich-media ads.

Guerrilla marketing: An unconventional way of performing promotional activities on a low budget, relying more on time, energy and imagination than a big marketing spend.

Hooks in books: A narrative inclusion that captures the reader's interest, e.g. by including recognisable character and place names.

IPRLicensing.co.uk: An international rights website which enables authors to list and sell the rights for their e-book to the world via a global network.

Kindle: The world's best-selling handheld e-reader (e-book reading device).

Kindleboards: Forum and discussion group facility available on Kindle to discuss and promote e-books.

Kobobooks.com: Major online retailer of e-books. *Kobo e-readers* are handheld e-book reading devices.

LinkedIn.com: Social networking website for people in professional occupations, such as publishing.

Look Inside!: A free facility offered by Amazon for you to show sample pages of your e-book to entice readers to buy your book.

Lovereading.com: The largest UK book club on the internet along with its partner site, Lovewriting.com, offering advice on publishing your work, and making it easy for people to sample, review and purchase your e-book.

Marketing campaign: The activities you undertake to raise your literary profile as a published author and promote and sell copies of your book.

Mass-Ebooks.com: A website offering free e-book downloads.

Media kit/press pack: A collection of marketing materials including a press release, author brief, fact sheet about your book, current news, suggested interview Q & As and your contact details which can be sent to the media to publicise your book.

Ning.com: A social networking site enabling you to create your own social networking site based on a particular subject, such as your e-book.

Nook: Hand-held electronic book reader developed by American book retailer Barnes & Noble.

Offline marketing: Traditional methods of marketing such as television/newspaper/magazine adverts, billboards, posters, jingles, etc.

Online marketing (*webvertising* or *e-marketing*): The promotion of products like e-books over the internet through search engine marketing and optimisation, social media, affiliate marketing, pay-per-click and banner ads, and e-mail marketing.

Outposts: Developing your social media postings to help attract your target audience and build brand recognition for your e-books.

Paypal.com: A global e-commerce business allowing payments and money transfers to be made through the Internet. Online money transfers serve as electronic alternatives to paying with traditional paper methods, such as checks and money orders.

Pay-per-click (PPC) advertising: A form of online marketing where you bid on specific key words and key word phrases relevant to your website or e-book so when someone puts those words into an internet search engine, banners and links are provided to your website. Each time someone clicks on these banners or links and are directed to your website, you pay a small fee to the PPC advertiser.

Plaxo.com: An online address book and social networking service.

Podcasting: Recording videos and making them available on the internet to anyone with a speedy internet connection.

Press release: Short (typically one or two pages) announcement of newsworthy events associated with your book.

PR websites/newswires: Distributors for press releases on the internet.

Publishing platform (for e-books): An e-publishing platform that allows the management of content, the definition of digital rights, authentication scenarios, the management of customers and e-commerce transactions, and the incorporation of marketing tools and text retrieval.

Reciprocal links: A mutually-agreed link between your website and another site intended to increase the numbers of visitors to both sites, and thereby achieve higher ranking on search engines, giving your site more prominence and (hopefully) your e-book more sales.

Ryze.com: Free social networking website designed to link business professionals and entrepreneurs.

Scribd.com: A digital documents library that allows users to publish, discover, share and discuss original writings in various languages. Allows users to post documents in various formats and embed them into a web page.

Search engine optimisation: Tailoring your website so when people search online for subjects related to your book on various browsers such like Google and Yahoo, they might find and access your website.

Shelfari.com: A social cataloguing website for books. Users build virtual bookshelves of titles they own or have read and can rate, review, tag, discuss and recommend books to others.

Smashwords.com: A DIY e-book self-publishing and distribution platform.

Social Bookmarking: A service on the internet for storing, sharing and discovering popular content. Instead of saving website links to your web browser, you save them to the web. Because your bookmarks are online, you can easily share them with friends.

Social media: Web- and mobile-based technologies to turn communication into interactive dialogue among organisations, communities, and individuals. This includes internet forums, weblogs, social blogs, micro-blogging, wikis, social networks, podcasts and social bookmarking.

Social networking: Expanding your contacts by making connections through attending events and meeting individuals. On the internet, establishing interconnected communities (commonly known as personal networks) that help people make contacts that would be good for them to know.

Target market: A group of people identified as those most likely to buy your book.

Thumbnail: Reduced-size versions of pictures, used to help in recognising and organising them.

Tradebit.com: Offers bandwidth/traffic to anybody who wants to sell e-book downloads and files online (with PayPal, Google Checkout or Clickbank).

Twitter.com: A free web-based service enabling its users to send and read text-based messages of up to 140 characters, known as *tweets*.

Typepad: Online service for hosting and publishing weblogs and photo albums, and supports a LinkedIn application that pulls blog posts into LinkedIn.

URL (uniform research locator)/domain name: The internet address for your website, generally beginning with http://www or simply www. and ending with .com, .co.uk, .net., .org, and so on.

Video blogging (*vlogging* or *vidblogging*): A form of blogging where short videos are made regularly and often combine embedded video or a video link with supporting text, images, and other data.

Viral marketing: Increasing awareness of you as a published author and your e-book through people talking about your e-book and recommending it to others.

WeRead.com: A popular online community of book enthusiasts.

Word of mouse marketing: Using social media sites on the internet to create a buzz about your e-book.

Word of mouth marketing (*see – Viral marketing*): Speaking with people and groups of people directly to create a following for your book.

Wordpress.com: A free and open source blogging tool.

YouTube: A video-sharing website on which users can upload, share and view videos, enabling authors to showcase themselves and their books.

Zinepal.com: Enables authors to create e-books from online content or read e-books created by others.

Some other titles from How To Books

LIKELY STORIES
Fabulous, inspirational, chuckleworthy and deeply instructive tales about creative
writing as told to the author by his ubiquitous Guru
HUGH SCOTT
Whitbread winning author

Originally published as articles in the *Writers' Forum* magazine, these tales tell of the
author's adventures when he meets his Guru, a fabulous and wise Being who appears
in many guises and who guides his pupil in the sometimes bewildering ways of creative
writing. Each story covers an aspect of creative writing such as character, dialogue,
atmosphere, writers' block, vocabulary, etc.

ISBN 978-1-84528-461-8

CHOOSE THE RIGHT WORD
An entertaining and easy-to-use guide to better English – with 70 test-yourself quizzes
ROBIN HOSIE & VIC MAYHEW

Light-hearted does not have to mean lightweight. *Choose the Right Word* sets out the
commonsense, if sometimes confusing, rules of the English language without resorting
to the tedium of technical terms that are understood only by professional
grammarians. It is a valuable source of reference for people whose grammar may have
become a little rusty over the years, and the quizzes help them to measure progress at
their own rate. This entertaining, reliable and easy-to-use guide to better English
features guidance on grammar rules and when they can be bent; spelling and
pronunciation tips; fun facts; and around 70 test-yourself quizzes.

ISBN 978-1-84528-499-2

365 WAYS TO GET YOU WRITING
Inspiration and advice for creative writers on a daily basis
JANE COOPER

This book will bring you a year's advice and inspiration to move your writing forward
on a regular basis. Each two-page spread opens with learning points and advice,
followed by interesting exercises to help you create believable characters; write realistic
dialogue; improve your writing through reading; use personal experience to inspire
fiction; find the factors that get a story going; choose the right tense and person for
your stories; show, rather than tell; and work out which writing rules really matter –
and follow them.

ISBN 978-1-84528-461-8